COLLEGE
CASH

VAN
HUTCHINSON

A Harvest/HBJ Original

COLLEGE CASH

How to Earn and Learn as a Student Entrepreneur

With illustrations by John Callahan

HARCOURT BRACE JOVANOVICH, PUBLISHERS
San Diego   New York   London

Illustrations reprinted by permission of John Callahan, copyright 1987.
Graph on p. 121 reprinted by permission of Junior Achievement, Inc.

Library of Congress Cataloging-in-Publication Data

Hutchinson, Van.
College cash.

"A Harvest/HBJ book."
Bibliography: p.
1. New business enterprises—United States.
2. Entrepreneur.
3. College students—Employment—United States.
I. Title.
HD62.5.H88   1988   658.4'2   87-8666
ISBN 0-15-619150-4 (pbk.)

Designed by Ann Smith
Printed in the United States of America
First Harvest/HBJ edition
A B C D E F G H I J

Contents

Foreword   **ix**

Verne Harnish, Co-founder, Association of
Collegiate Entrepreneurs

1 Launching a Megatrend   **1**

The Student Entrepreneur Movement in America

***California Dreamin'* Featuring Dan
Bienenfeld of Design Look, Inc.**

Are You an Entrepreneur? (A Quiz) ● Rewards of
Entrepreneurship

2 Follow Your Heart—Using Your Head   **13**

Choosing the Right Business for You

***Free and Clear* Featuring Marc Magor of
High Adventure Sports**

Take Your Passion ● Make It Happen ● Testing
the Market ● Entrepreneur Apprenticeship ●
Brainstorming ● Making the Decision ● 50 Proven
Business Ideas for Students

3 Plan Your Work, Work Your Plan   **27**

Creating and Using a Business Plan

***Cooking Up Cash* Featuring Ken Carter of
T. C. Catering**

Researching Your Idea ● Choosing a Name ● The
Business Plan ● Putting Your Business Plan to Work

4 Capitalizing on a Shoestring   **49**

How to Find Those Hidden Resources

***Becoming an EntrepRENOIR* Featuring Beth
Whiting of All Beth's Creations**

v

Your Initial Operating Budget ● Finding Startup
Money ● Obtaining a Loan ● Location ● Buying
Equipment, Services, and Supplies ● Surviving
Startup

5 Use a Rifle, Not a Shotgun 65
Finding All the Customers You Can Handle
Getting Rich Featuring Kim Merritt of Kim's
Khocolate, Inc.

Defining Your Market ● Co-Evolving with Your
Competitors ● Pricing and Packaging ● Test
Marketing ● Alternative Marketing Strategies

6 When It Pays to Be Off the Wall 79
Advertising, Promotions, and Publicity
Clowning Around Featuring Jim Hall,
Professional Entertainer

Printed Sales Tools ● Paid Advertising ● Publicity
(Free Advertising!) ● Promotions ● Word-of-Mouth
Advertising Networks ● 30 Creative Advertising
Ideas

7 From "Thanks, But—" to "Yes, Please!" 93
How to Open and Close a Sale
Pondering Profits Featuring Don Carruthers
of Food For Thought

New Age Principles for Sales Success ● The
Psychology of Selling ● Overcoming Objections ●
Followup ● A Few Final Sales Tips

8 Laughing All the Way to the Bank 109
Bookkeeping and Cash Management
Playing Anti-Monopoly Featuring Ken
Appel of KB Books

Bookkeeping Systems ● Receipts and Other Paper
Records ● Billing ● Banking ● Am I Really Making
Money? ● Break-Even Point ● Getting Advice ●
Selling Your Business

9 Sam's Your Uncle, Not Your Big Brother   **123**
A Demystification of Legal and Tax Concerns
Taking It to the Street Featuring Dave and
Stephen Goldman of MacProducts USA

Legal Paperwork: The Basics ● Facts about Taxes ●
Deductions for Student Entrepreneurs ● Filling Out
the Forms ● Help!

10 Managing the Win/Win Way   **141**
New Styles of Entrepreneurial Leadership
Summing Up the Parts Featuring Karl
Edelmann of Edelkinder GMBH

Sole Proprietorship ● Partnership ● The
Entrepreneurial Team ● Evaluating Your Needs ●
The New Management School ● Creating the Team

11 The Business Physician's Desk Reference   **161**
What to Do When Your Business Gets a Cold
On-Line Adventure Featuring David Fogel
of Hotline Software

Nine Diseases Common to Student Businesses ●
Preventive Medicine

12 Time Flies—Fly with It!   **177**
Time Management and Motivation
Speaking from the Heart Featuring Laurie
Stewart of L. A. Stewart Productions

The Sequence for Success ● Managing Blocks of
Time ● Balancing School and Business Activities ●
Staying Motivated ● Empowering Habits for High
Achievement

13 Readin' Writin' and Retail   **193**
How to Integrate School and Entrepreneurship
Hot-Wiring Reality Featuring Brett
Kingstone, Author

Academic Credit ● Entrepreneurship Programs ●
Other Training Programs ● Ace—The Association of
Collegiate Entrepreneurs ● Entrepreneurial Education
in Perspective ● Start an Entrepreneurs' Club

14 **Spaceship Earth/Destination: Enterprise** **209**
Entrepreneurship in the New Age
New Age Networking **Featuring Scott Mize**
of Mize Technology Development

Social Transformation through Business ● What
Wealth Really Is ● A Vision for the Future . . . and
Where We Are Now

Appendix A: Resources **225**

Appendix B: Entrepreneurial Ideas **228**

Appendix C: Business Plan and Budget **236**

Acknowledgments **239**

About the Author **240**

About the Illustrator **241**

Foreword

"Things may come to those who wait, but only the things left by those who hustle."

Abraham Lincoln

On February 23, 1886, a young man working in his basement completed the development of a process which would pave the way for the technological revolution. The young man was 22-year-old Charles Hall and the process was the world's first commercially viable method for extracting aluminum. He would later launch the Aluminum Company of America—better known today as ALCOA.

Roughly a hundred years later a handful of college students—each with something of Charles Hall's spirit—gathered in the basement of a Chinese restaurant in Harvard Square. We came together to consolidate a movement that had begun on campus and among young people all across our nation—entrepreneurship. That evening marked the birth of what has become an international association for young and collegiate entrepreneurs, the Association of Collegiate Entrepreneurs.

It has been nearly a century since the world has witnessed the kind of explosive interest in entrepreneurship we see today among our nation's young people. With one-third of all new businesses being created by people age 30 and under, credit for the fivefold increase in yearly new business startups over the past decade is shared by the youth of our nation. As in the past, young people are leading a revolution important to our nation and the world.

To quote *Time* magazine, "Perhaps it is not an overstatement to say that the future economic salvation of the global economy lies in the hands of the entrepreneur." Our work with young entrepreneurs and students throughout 23 countries has convinced us that the future lies with those who embrace an entrepreneurial vision. Whether you put it to work starting your own venture or effecting change within existing organizations, remember the bottom line—those who fail to embrace entrepreneurship will serve those who do!

Start a venture on your own! I wish I could personally reach out from these pages and convince you that the time is now to exercise your entrepreneurial spirit. If only you could meet some of the "Top 100" young entrepreneurs we honor—last year their combined gross revenues exceeded $2 billion—you would feel the energy and excitement that's building. Things are moving fast—there couldn't be a better time to get moving.

Which is why we are excited about Van's book. It is only appropriate that the author of a book showing others how to start their own business is the quintessential collegiate entrepreneur himself. Starting with an "organic lemonade" operation at age six, Van has been in the trenches "doing deals" and running his own businesses ever since.

A prolific writer, Van has been (and continues to be) a columnist for several youth magazines. He wrote his first book at age 18. He is a speaker as well, and has given hundreds of seminars at schools and university groups—including three well received talks at our ACE International Conventions. We were very honored when Van took the time to establish an ACE entrepreneur group on his own campus, at the University of California, San Diego.

Van has an uncanny ability to draw valuable information from successful individuals and then synthesize it in an entertaining, accessible way. And he does it with passion, enthusiasm, and a desire to help others turn their dreams to reality. I know you'll enjoy Van's book—he has provided here the knowledge required to take the first step. Now it's up to you.

Verne Harnish, Co-founder
Association of Collegiate Entrepreneurs

Until one is committed, there is hesitating, the chance to draw back, always ineffectiveness. . . The moment one definitely commits oneself, Providence moves, too. . . .

A whole stream of events issues from the decision, raising in one's favor all manner of unforeseen incidents, and meetings, and material assistance. . . .

Whatever you can do or dream you can do, begin it. Boldness has genius, power, and magic in it. Begin it now.

— Goethe

COLLEGE CASH

1
LAUNCHING A MEGATREND
The Student Entrepreneur Movement in America

"Transition times between economies are the
times when entrepreneurship blooms.
We are now in such a period."
–John Naisbitt,
Megatrends

CALIFORNIA DREAMIN'

featuring
Dan Bienenfeld of Design Look, Inc.

They've got everything you'd ever want to cuddle.
Kittens. Teddy Bears. Hard bodies. Soft curves. Such
motifs make up a line of 26 calendars produced by
Dan Bienenfeld of Design Look, Inc.

At age 21, Dan Bienenfeld is one of the greatest
success stories in entrepreneurial history, and has
been recognized in the *Wall Street Journal* and
Woman's Day. Dan began his company, originally
College Look Publications, in his freshman year at
the University of California, Santa Barbara (UCSB).
His first calendar, "The Men of UC Santa Barbara," brought in $10,000. The next year Dan joined
forces with two other successful student entrepreneurs, Sam Angus (a student stock broker and ten-
nis pro) and Chip Conk (a model), and established
a corporation.

Armed with past success, they decided to go for
"Legs." It was a sensational hit. That and future
calendar ideas inspired them to go for major capital. "We brainstormed a list of every millionaire
we knew and put together a pseudo business plan.
It was kind of a joke." Nonetheless, the first person
they approached gave them $80,000 in capital. They
set to work immediately producing "California

Dreamin'," a glossy hunk calendar that drove schoolgirls to lust.

Sales jumped to $200,000, then $400,000 the succeeding year. It topped a million in 1986. With a phalanx of 154 American sales representatives and 29 in Canada to generate excitement, Dan captured a good share of a fickle market. In the company's third year, Chip Conk left to start his own venture. After his departure, Dan and Sam put together a deal with Warner Brothers to produce "The Exclusive Madonna Calendar." "That calendar not only brought in revenue," Dan declares jubilantly, "its main purpose was to establish us in the industry."

Entrepreneurship has always been a part of Dan's academic life. He cofounded the entrepreneur's club at University of California, Santa Barbara; it became the largest student organization on campus two months after its inception. As a freshman, he opened up an aerobic dance studio in a local church and hired others to do the teaching. "Once," he remembers, "one of the teachers didn't show up and I had to play Jack LaLanne. It was hilarious. Two of the ladies decided that instead of letting me make a fool of myself, they would come up and aid and abet me."

Design Look's million-dollar sales typify the kind of results the current generation of young entrepreneurs are attaining through commitment and drive. Dan insists that the reason he and his partners got the money was "*not* because of our business plan. It was because of our energy. If you want

anybody to believe in you, especially financial partners, you've got to prove you're a committed individual, that you're willing to give up your
summer, or give up six months—give it 100 percent—and put yourself completely on the line."

We young people are among the most creative,
motivated, adaptable, and dynamic human beings
there are. We have the energy and creativity to transform
ideas in our heads into profits in our hands. Many students
are already doing it.

At the University of Texas, Austin, a 23-year-old senior
student entrepreneur named David Goldman and his brother
Stephen, age 22, are running a computer accessories store
that grosses $250,000 a month. Sales will top $4 million
before they graduate.

In Cincinnati, Ohio, 20-year-old Beth Whiting began
painting jewelry for fun. Her hobby turned into a $10,000-
a-year business that she still is able to conduct in her spare
time.

Today about three-quarters of a million people under
age 30 all over the U.S. are running their own businesses.
A good share of them are college students who manage
their businesses in between classes and during vacations.
One builds doghouses in Alaska. One sells sunglasses in
California. Another designs swimwear in Florida. Some of
these enterprises will add valuable and interesting experience to students' résumés. Other student businesses may
become the next IBM or Apple.

Enterprising college students are bringing new spirit to
an old word, *entrepreneur*. Its roots are French *entre-*

prendre, meaning "to undertake: to take a risk." Every student featured in this book is living in this bold new spirit. They are rightly called *entrepreneurs*: ones who conceive, create, and take the ultimate risk of a business venture.

As the 1980s move into the 1990s, more and more students are taking responsibility for their futures. Where "Let it be" was the campus motto in the 1970s, "Make it happen" has become the theme of a generation of students bent on "making it" before age 30. In a *Wall Street Journal* article headlined "On campuses, making the Dean's List comes second to making a profit," Karen Blumenthal wrote, "College students, once given to burning draft cards, are increasingly exchanging business cards." Further, she saw this generation's entrepreneurial fervor as "a reaffirmation of belief in the nation as a land of opportunity."

Entrepreneurship among students is more than a trend, more than a fad. One business journal called it "a major movement sweeping American college campuses today." In one sense, student entrepreneurs are not totally new; the high school student with a lawn route and the freelance typist have been perennial fixtures on campus. But student entrepreneurs of the late 1980s are far more sophisticated. And there are scads more of them.

Why a student entrepreneur movement now? Several reasons: First, today's student entrepreneurs are selling to a generation that has more money and sophistication than any other in recent American history. By some estimates the college market is still a virtually untapped economic frontier worth from $30 to $100 billion a year.

Time has called this decade "The Roaring '80s" and the prevailing mood of prosperity and optimism has encouraged new enterprises. The number of new businesses registered in 1985 was more than triple that of 1960, and *more than 30 percent of these were begun by entrepreneurs under age 30.*

Second, rising college costs have served as an incentive for students to earn their way through school creatively. One student entrepreneur sums up simply, "There's no way in the world I could put myself through school if I were still a slave in some minimum-wage job."

Third, the communication revolution has made it possible for virtually anyone to become an entrepreneur. The personal computer has proven to be a gold mine for those long on creativity and short on capital. Student computer whizzes—some of them not old enough to drive anything but a disk—have amazed the world with their computer-based enterprises.

Even indirectly, the communication revolution is fueling the fire of entrepreneurship: "The 'New-Person network' of young entrepreneurial people has nothing to do with the 'Old Boy network'—the families who've had money for centuries," says 28-year-old author Brett Kingstone. "Nowadays, things are based more on a *meritocracy*, rather than an aristocracy."

Fourth, entrepreneurship offers endless possibilities in a competitive job market that forces even highly qualified applicants to accept jobs in fields that don't interest them. Verne Harnish, energetic co-founder of the Association of Collegiate Entrepreneurs, advises: "When you can't find a job, you'd better go *make* one!" Entrepreneurship is an escape hatch for those of us too ambitious to stand in the welfare line, too creative to let ourselves get jammed into institutional pigeonholes.

Traditionally, being a student meant being excluded

from the mainstream economy. Entrepreneurship offers students a way to profit directly from their own labor. Beth Whiting speaks plainly: "We want something we can call our own."

The new attitude among late– and post–Baby Boomers indicates a resurgency of American individualism. "We're seeing more and more students who simply aren't interested in going to work in the corporate world," Fran Jabara told *INC.* magazine recently. A well-known proponent of the student entrepreneur movement, Dr. Jabara notes that today's students "saw their dads working only for Fridays, vacations, and retirement—and not being very happy as a result."

The new student entrepreneurs are looking for better opportunities, for their own dreams to pursue. And they're beginning to change the way America does business. Their companies are less bureaucratic—more flexibly managed—and place greater emphasis on employee participation and ownership. Very often they're more profitable than older, more entrenched companies. Verne Harnish observes, "This bunch doesn't just try to apply *In Search of Excellence*-type concepts—they do it by instinct!"

There's no question about it: The time is right to be a student entrepreneur. The real question is: Are *you* ready?

To be a student entrepreneur, you must be a special kind of person. Running a business takes more than just showing up for work in the morning and filling out a W–2 form. It requires so much creativity, independence, people-sense, and persistence that most students go running for the first minimum-wage job they can find.

Maybe you're different. The following questionnaire can give you an idea.

ARE YOU AN ENTREPRENEUR?
A QUIZ

(Give yourself a point for each "yes.")

1. Did you ever have a lemonade stand or similar enterprise as a kid?

2. Did you ever have a paper route or sell things door-to-door?

3. Are your parents, siblings, or extended family members entrepreneurs?

4. Do you have a number of ideal businesses you'd like to start? Or one big dream venture in the back of your mind?

5. Do you bite your nails, talk rapidly, or have a "Type A" personality?

6. Have you ever quit or been fired from a job because you thought it should be done differently?

7. Do you do better in school subjects that involve creative thinking?

8. Are you highly independent?

9. Are you good at persuading people or selling things?

10. Do you believe in yourself no matter what happens, and have the will to master any situation?

Scoring

0–1 Have you considered slavery?

2–3 Check the "Help Wanted" ads.

4–5 Get together with some other entrepreneurial-minded people and make a plan.

6–8 Don't delay. Start immediately!

9–10 Visit a Wall Street venture capitalist today for a $1,000,000 loan! (See note.)

This questionnaire singles out a few of the traits common to student entrepreneurs who—by the way—come from every economic background, every educational background, every geographic region, every ethnic group, and both sexes. However, the characteristics listed in the questionnaire have been shown to correlate somewhat with the entrepreneurial personality.

Some other qualities are vital for successful entrepreneurs:

Creativity Entrepreneurs are innovators. Their brains are typically buzzing with new products to design and new

---

NOTE: If you checked "yes" to number 10, ignore the rest. It is the only item on the questionnaire that ultimately makes any difference whatsoever. If you have the will to succeed, you *will* master every situation. Never ask, "Do I *have* what it takes?" Ask, "Am I willing to *go get* what it takes?"

marketing concepts to test out. Twenty-year-old Kim Merritt owns a chocolate business that thrives because she has created styles of chocolate even Lady Godiva hasn't dreamed of; 24-year-old David Fogel found a way to put Sherlock Holmes mysteries on disks.

Independence   Personality tests show entrepreneurs to be stubborn individuals who often start businesses to show they can do it better than their past employers. Marc Magor got fed up working for a fraction of the fees charged by his old employer, Lake Michigan Wind Sports, and began his own hang gliding instruction company. His old employer went out of business soon after.

People-sense   In running a business—where success is completely dependent on people—people-sense is just as important as cents-sense. Developing good interpersonal skills is so important that Laurie Stewart makes them the focus of many of her success seminars for college groups and companies.

Persistence   On receiving his first social security check at age 65, one entrepreneur was chagrined to find it barely enough to buy a bird for his frying pan. Boldly he set out to find someone to buy and market his bird batter. He was rebuffed not once or twice, but 1008 times! On the 1009th sales pitch, a bidder finally bit the bait. The entrepreneur's persistence led to the nationwide phenomenon known as Kentucky Fried Chicken. Not a bad bit of bartering.

The moral of the story: Bust your butt if you believe you're better.

REWARDS OF ENTREPRENEURSHIP

Imagine starting a business that grosses over $1 million a year, like Design Look, Inc. Or clearing $3,000 in a month, as Kim Merritt did from a single chocolate contract. If you need to put yourself through school or help support your family, starting a business can move you far out of the minimum-wage league.

And that's just the money, which isn't even the prime motivator of entrepreneurs. Ambition, challenge, and the need to be independent are the forces that really drive an entrepreneur. A business of your own offers an alternative to playing "go-fer" for someone else. Why not go for goals you set yourself? Believe me, as a freelance writer and speaker, there's nothing I value more than the freedom to make my own decisions, schedule my own time, and not have any boss other than myself to answer to.

Third, as a student entrepreneur, you can earn and learn at the same time. Brett Kingstone learned so much from his entrepreneurial pursuits during college that he wrote *The Student Entrepreneur's Guide* before graduating from Stanford. You can learn much from your own business that will serve you in many of your academic projects.

Finally, the common reward shared by all the successful student entrepreneurs I interviewed was a deep-down, inside-the-skin satisfaction. Offering the world a well-made product or a needed service is where it starts; becoming a better you it where it ends. This world doesn't need another sullen worker trudging to his or her routine position in the assembly line. It needs more turned-on human beings.

2

FOLLOW YOUR HEART— USING YOUR HEAD

Choosing the Right Business for You

"He who has a *why* to live for can bear with almost any *how*."
—Friedrich Wilhelm Nietzsche

FREE AND CLEAR

featuring
Marc Magor of High Adventure Sports

To Marc Magor, the very essence of being an entrepreneur is freedom. Freedom to set his own hours, freedom to dictate his own operating rules, and freedom to spread his wings and literally soar with the seagulls.

Operating his own hang gliding instruction business has been a dream since childhood. He says, "I knew. I just knew that I was meant to be flying and bringing that experience to other people." He also knew that entrepreneurship was the only way for him. He states, "I can't handle working for someone. It's like being grounded. It's like selling your life."

Marc has been in this young sport since the days when people built their own hang gliders out of bamboo and polyethylene—garbage bag material. After serving as a hired instructor for Lake Michigan Wind Sports, a hang gliding school near South Bend, Indiana, he started his own school, High Adventure Sports.

His first task was to get equipment: four hang gliders, harnesses, and helmets, which he bought on credit from his former employer. Marc and a partner began training students on the same Lake

Michigan sand dune as the other company. Lake Michigan Wind Sports went out of business later that season.

At High Adventure Sports, business soared. At $65 per student for a full-day lesson, the company was making good money. New customers learned about it from a billboard by the park and the Chicago Yellow Pages, but mainly from word-of-mouth publicity. After two summer seasons, High Adventure Sports had netted about $14,000.

During his second season in business, Marc had an inspiration. Since most of southwest Michigan and northern Indiana is flat farmland, launching oneself in a hang glider from a mountaintop is about as likely as surfing in Oklahoma. "Why not," thought Marc, "tow up the pilot and glider the way you'd fly a kite?" A little research confirmed that safe methods using a car, a winch, and a tow tope were being used with success. He wasted no time converting his old Dodge into a towing vehicle. With the help of his physics professor at Indiana University, he rigged a quick-release system on the hang glider whereby the pilot could release the tow cable after climbing to about a thousand feet of altitude.

Marc is still perfecting this method, which he hopes will revolutionize hang gliding in the Midwest. For obvious reasons, he wants to make sure it is completely safe before he starts using it commercially, but he has absolute confidence in it. He affirms, "If you can conceptualize it, you can achieve it."

It was a snowy evening in Kalamazoo, Michigan. I was riding with my friend Laurie Stewart to a Toast-masters meeting when the theme song to the movie *Flash-dance* came on the radio. The beat and the idea of turning one's passion into a reality made us tap our feet and sing with it. Laurie turned to me and said, "You know, Van, I really like that song. It makes me feel great about what I'm doing. I think I'll work that into my speech."

The speech turned out great. Her business turned out better. Speaking was something Laurie loved to do, and she found a way to market it. After years of apprenticeship, she now makes $500 to $1,000 per speech. Laurie took her passion and made it happen.

Coming up with the Great American Business Idea is the essence of being an entrepreneur. For some, the idea comes like a bolt of lightning. (Incidentally, Ben Franklin—the quintessential American entrepreneur—was reportedly struck by lightning several times. Perhaps this accounts for his myriad inventions!) For others, their enterprises are an adaptation of an idea from another part of the world. Still others find themselves in business by accident. In all cases, the ideal business idea is one which:

1. *You* enjoy doing.
2. People need *and* are willing to pay for.

Keep these two criteria in mind as you decide on a business to try. Together, profit and fun seem to multiply exponentially. One without the other means either bore-dom or zero cash flow—and either way, failure.

STEP 1: TAKE YOUR PASSION . . .
Entrepreneurs all seem to create businesses out of things they enjoy doing. To all of them, work is play. No wonder entrepreneurs put in such long hours!

Marc Magor is a perfect example. To him, there is no better thrill than introducing students to the freedom of flight, except for flying tandem—side-by-side in the same hang glider—with one of his students along Lake Michigan near South Bend, Indiana. Through his summer business, High Adventure Sports, Marc is doing exactly what he loves to do.

For others, the "play" aspect is not so much in the activity itself, but is the thrill of risking and making money. Speculative entrepreneurs thrive on the dips and dives of economic roller coasters. Still others derive pleasure from mixing with types who play high-level investment and leveraged buyout games. To these people, the entrepreneurial world offers real-life excitement and real, live dollars . . . TV just offers "Dallas."

Why not make the same Work-Is-Play ideal work for you? It starts with understanding yourself. What do you really like to do? Do you like to design and build things? Sell items to people? Make crafts or artwork? Sing, speak, or. act? Fix things? Tutor or work with children? Train animals? Organize productive labor? Write poetry, prose, or computer programs? Think like an entrepreneur thinks: "How can I take what I've got and turn it into an opportunity?"

STEP 2: . . . MAKE IT HAPPEN

A good idea not only has to be enjoyable, it has to be marketable. It should meet these criteria:

1. It must fill a need.

2. The need must be perceived (everyone needs education, for example, but not everyone perceives the need for it).

3. It must be convenient, priced right, and packaged attractively (see Chapter 5).

4. It must fill a niche not already overrun by competition (see Chapter 5).

5. It should add value to the human experience. People may have a perceived "need" to fill their lungs with smoke, fill their gullets with junk food, and fill their minds with trash, but I don't see these as true human needs that need filling. Don't waste your time and your incredible human potential by speeding others to destruction. Offer something that helps develop the human spirit, not something that kills it.*

A. David Silver, author of *Entrepreneurial Megabucks,* tells his seminar audiences that the greatest enterprises are founded on ideas that fill a basic human need in a dramatic way. He advises young entrepreneurs to find enterprising ways to fight world hunger, build better housing, etc. "Whoever finds a cure for AIDS is going to be very rich," Silver comments.

TESTING THE MARKET

Which business ideas will meet these criteria? Keep your eyes, ears, and mind open. Here are some ways to check the market pulse.

---

* People asked me why I didn't feature drug dealers in my book. After all, they said, dealing dope is a venerable and time-honored student enterprise. Besides, they said, dealers also make scads of money—and they practically invented multilevel marketing.

If turning a 12-year-old into a dealer so he can shake down other kids on the playground is "multilevel marketing," then pimps might as well be called "personnel managers." Don't buy into our culture's habit for equating success with money alone. *True* success is creating a venture that enriches *all* parties involved.

Talk to friends, neighbors, and relatives. A chat over the backyard fence or a morning's worth of calls may reveal neighbors who need house painting, lawn mowing, or shrub trimming. One easy, high-profit business for students, especially in new housing developments, is painting house numbers on street curbs.

Talk to small business owners. Small businesses require a million tasks yet few owners have time to do them. Offer to help small businesspersons maintain their professional image—and sanity—with a service like after-hours cleanup, promotional posters and banners, custom computer software design, or delivery services. Large institutions like schools, hospitals, or corporations sometimes subcontract to students who approach them professionally.

Read widely. Entrepreneurially oriented books, as well as magazines like *Entrepreneur*, *Venture*, *Success*—or more specialized magazines like *Popular Mechanics*—can be great idea stimulators. Get a hold of Brett Kingstone's books, *The Student Entrepreneur's Guide* and *The Dynamos: Who Are They Anyway?* City or campus newspapers and magazines like *Dorm* and *Newsweek on Campus* can help you keep abreast of fads and trends. (A useful list of books, magazines, and other resources is given in Appendix A.)

Travel. Marco Polo's medieval junket to the Orient opened up a whole new era of trade. Your road trip to Podunk University across the state might not revolutionize the world economy, but it just might cross-fertilize your awareness of what's successful on other campuses.

Get to an ACE conference. At a regional or international conference of the Association of Collegiate Entrepreneurs you can get a very specific idea of what the market is—by seeing what other entrepreneurs are doing.

Talk to other students. Why not discover and fill the needs of the group you know best? The market is specialized, close at hand, and often unrecognized by Big Business. Starting with your friends, conduct a small survey like this one.

> What products or services on campus do you feel are overpriced?
>
> What student needs are not met at all?
>
> What kinds of student-run enterprises would you like to see on campus?
>
> When was the last time you said to yourself, "What this campus really needs is a . . . "?

CALLAHAN

"One last question: Where are you?"

ENTREPRENEUR APPRENTICESHIP
(AN ALTERNATIVE TO "THE PLUNGE")

Entrepreneurship is typically labeled as a risky, go-it-alone affair. It doesn't have to be. There are many ways to get your feet wet before taking the entrepreneurial plunge. Here are just three:

Work for an employer in the field you want to explore. Learn everything you can and ask every question you can think of.

Continue and expand a family business. The five Edelmann children began producing an automotive product their father had carried, and each of the five profited by $4000 the first year. If your family ever has had a cottage industry like chopping and selling firewood or making Christmas tree ornaments, consider picking up where the family left off.

Expand a club project. Organizations like Junior Achievement, Future Farmers of America (FFA), and Future Business Leaders of America (FBLA) teach students about businesses at the high school level.

At the college level, campus entrepreneurs' clubs help students launch many new enterprises. If you join one (or start one), you'll exchange so many ideas with other student entrepreneurs you'll be tempted to start not one, but several businesses—immediately!

BRAINSTORMING: THE ULTIMATE SOURCE OF
ENTREPRENEURIAL IDEAS

Brainstorming to an entrepreneur is like Kim's Khocolate to a fudge fiend: Addicting. In brainstorming, the whole object is to come up with as many ideas as possible in a short period of time. The absolute rule is that *every* idea, no matter how silly, gets written down, and no idea is judged before its time. (These "silly" ideas can often lead to the innovative concept that makes a million.) The serious evaluation comes later, after you've filled sheets of paper with ideas.

Try brainstorming. Grab a pen, take a deep breath, and go for it! See how many creative ideas you can come up with in ten minutes. If you start to slow down, refer to the list of proven student enterprises. Whatever happens, don't take your pen from the paper. You might not be able to stop! (In fact, it might become a lifelong habit.)

MAKING THE DECISION

The first time I jumped off a cliff, I stood on the edge a long time. I looked at the rocks and churning waves below and thought carefully. Then I leaped out into space.

Deciding on the right business enterprise is a lot like my first cliff-launch with a hang glider, which I just described. It's not a snap decision. Like gaining altitude in a booming thermal of rising air in the desert, you could get incredibly high from a profitable decision. You also could crash. But at least you aren't sitting there on the ground too fearful to fly! Whether deciding to fly or deciding to start a business, think carefully first.

Consult other people. Seek advice and encouragement *only* from people you respect. Other entrepreneurs and entrepreneurial-minded instructors and advisors typically have the soundest advice. Parents can be the best source of inspiration, providing they believe in you and give you the freedom to fly or fail. But beware: families are often well-meaning pillows of "smother-love" which stifle the entrepreneurial spirit. Many great ideas have been aborted when would-be entrepreneurs heeded those who whined "It'll never work," "You're too young," or the classic "But we've never done it that way before!" Keep pessimists at an electric cattle prod's length. Pay attention to your gut feeling or answers to prayer. (Entrepreneurship and faith have a lot in common.) Believe in your own dream, and follow the advice of Steve Jobs, formerly of Apple Computer, who once told a convention of young entrepreneurs, "Follow your heart, *using your head*."

50 PROVEN BUSINESS IDEAS FOR STUDENTS

All of the ideas listed in this section are actual operating businesses being run by college students across the U.S. Most of them can be started with little training or capital. These ideas, along with more ambitious or specialized enterprises, are classified in Appendix B.

Mow lawns

Wash windows and clean screens

Paint address numbers on curbs

Paint houses

Cut and sell firewood

Design T-shirts or sweaters

Create custom artwork and advertising for businesses

Give art, music, or sports lessons

Tutor other students

Make and sell pastries or candy

Start an investment club/entrepreneurs' networking party

Write computer programs or act as a computer consultant

Start a message service on campus

Clean fireplaces

Build custom-designed lofts in dorm rooms

Clean and paint furniture

Clean swimming pools

Paint murals on buildings

Photograph weddings and special events

Sharpen tools and mower blades

Make and sell doghouses

Wash, groom, exercise, or train pets

Photograph pets

Type term papers

Tune up bicycles, cars, motorcycles, or small engines

Fix stereos and cassette players

Retrieve golf balls from ponds

Raise worms and fish bait

Baby-sit and care for children

House-sit for vacationers

Till gardens

Grow and sell flowers or vegetables, especially pumpkins for Halloween

Design and sew unusual children's clothing

Buy and sell used college books

Deliver snacks to dorm rooms

Make pizza for delivery or freezing

Photograph or videotape real estate

Photograph or videotape valuables for insurance records

Sell balloons at public events and parties

Wash and wax cars, boats, or airplanes

Cut and style hair

Organize children's parties and excursions

Market your own line of cookies, fudge, cakes, etc.

Start a dog poop cleanup service

Cater private picnics in remote or romantic spots

Compile a discount coupon book of local merchants

Make photo business cards

Deal in used computer equipment

Plow driveways or shovel snow off sidewalks

Seal driveways and paint lines on parking lots.

3

PLAN YOUR WORK, WORK YOUR PLAN

Creating and Using a Business Plan

"Those who fail to plan are planning to fail."
—Dr. Denis Waitley,
The Psychology of Winning

COOKING UP CASH

featuring
Ken Carter of T.C. Catering

The mayor of Gary, Indiana, had a problem. The city was full of young people with nothing to do, and he needed to come up with some city-sponsored (and publicly funded) activities to keep them out of trouble. A resourceful man, he went to the right source for answers—the kids themselves. When he posed the question to the then 14-year-old Ken Carter, who was serving on the mayor's Youth Advisory Board, Ken replied, "What young people want is work. I have a business that hires only teenagers. We're just looking for people to hire us."

The mayor liked Ken (and his solution to youth unemployment) so much that he contracted his company that weekend for a 50-person event. From then on, reports Ken, "I catered a lot for the mayor. I could use his name and I had clout."

T.C. Catering had been started about two years earlier. His very first job was almost bigger than he was—a 200-person wedding. But he didn't lack experience; he had been working at a catering company for six months. Ken remembers, "For the first two weeks, I didn't get a dime. Little did they know I'd soon be their competition."

Success at age 12 earned him a ticket to media fame. He was featured on a local TV show and was later interviewed for a three-page story in *Black Enterprise* magazine. When he was 15, he appeared on "The Phil Donahue Show." The associate producer was so impressed with Ken that she offered to be his media manager.

If running a business in college is a juggling act, then running one in high school is a three-ring circus. A 17-year-old junior at Horace Mann High School in Gary, Indiana, Ken often misses class to prepare for events for which he employs up to 30 people. One night he needed to organize his work force to cater two separate parties—each expecting over a thousand guests!

Like so many young entrepreneurs, Ken had to overcome the big problem of gaining credibility. He says, "People used to tell me, 'I'm a 45-year-old man and I can't find a job. So how do you think you're going to make it?' "

Ken can just smile and point to the results. To date, T.C. Catering has taken in over $30,000. Further down the road he plans to sell the business, or move to a major city like Chicago or Los Angeles. And he always keeps his big dream foremost in his mind—to own and operate a posh hotel in New Orleans. "I've always dreamed of being wealthy. It's just a matter of following your dream," he says with a smile.

After trying brainstorming and other ideas from the last chapter, you'll probably hit upon one you enjoy and that meets a market need. Take it from one who has been stricken by entrepreneurial fever many times: This is an exciting, chaotic time. Your head will be filled with ideas flying around and bumping into one another. The purpose of this chapter is to help you focus those ideas and turn them into a workable plan.

RESEARCHING YOUR IDEA

If you had unlimited time, money, and patience, you could learn everything you need to know about your business without research. Many people have the notion that the only way to learn is by trial and error—usually lots of error. Amoebas, three-toed sloths, and tax auditors learn the same way. Since you are a highly evolved human being, why not learn from *others'* mistakes and successes? Begin by checking out the field. Take notes on product prices or service options that your competition is offering. How could you make yours better? Who are their suppliers? What segments of the market are they going after? Make contacts with key people in the field. Your competition will often become your best contacts, especially if they are indirectly competitive or in another geographic region. Find a way to share ideas, contacts, and tips for getting started.

Research your idea in how-to books and magazines. Attend a seminar on starting a small business. Local Small Business Administration (SBA) offices schedule such seminars at least once a month. The best seminars are often found at conventions for student entrepreneurs, such as those sponsored by ACE. Other experienced entrepreneurs will be glad to share ideas, advice, and war stories. If you are taking any business courses at school, ask your professor for help in developing your particular entrepreneurial plan. The library is another valuable resource.

The best research comes from direct, hands-on market research: *Ask potential customers if they would buy the product or idea.* This could be one of the most important things you will ever do in business. Countless ideas have failed because overenthusiastic entrepreneurs assumed everyone would love their pet idea as much as they did. In the Soviet Union, where test marketing is unheard of, the Politburo thinks it knows what's best for the people. One time, a Soviet clothing plant decided to try competing with the Levis being sold on the black market. The plant manager declared, "*Our* blue jeans will not fade. Ours are not like those of the decadent Americans." The plant churned out truckload after truckload of perfect, unfadeable jeans.

No one bought them.

Test marketing is not as hard as it sounds. For example, if you are starting a campus food delivery service, knock on a number of doors in various dorms. Ask people if they would use the service, which hours would be convenient, what foods they would like, etc.

As you are collecting ideas for your business, jot them in an "idea notebook" or on a designated computer "idea disk." When the ideas are buzzing around you like flies, trap them and get them down in writing! They will prove invaluable when you sit down to actually plan the business.

CHOOSING A NAME

Naming your business should be done with as much thought as naming a child. After all, it may grow up to be the next Apple Computer Corp.

Make sure it reflects the image you want to present to your customers:

Local, personal, or convenient? (Kim's Khocolate, All Beth's Creations, etc.)

Hi-tech? (Hotline Software, Mize Technology Development, etc.)

Global? (Starr International, Edelkinder GMBH, etc.)

A catchy name can set the tone for advertising themes. A pair of painters named their business Paint Medics. They advertise a "free diagnosis" when the "health of your home is at stake."

THE BUSINESS PLAN

The more ideas you get, the more you'll probably want to plunge right into business. Beware! Some would-be entrepreneurs race into ventures without thinking first—and lose money, time, and customers. Poor planning also can cause a business to plod along at a slow rate of growth because of insufficient cash flow. Although you might occasionally strike it rich with plunging, or succeed eventually in a plodding business, planning will always yield the strongest, fastest growth.

A business plan is a written sketch of the basic elements of the business you're about to start. It is essential to gain other people's confidence in your plans, and venture capitalists won't even consider funding a business without one. Perhaps most importantly, organizing your business on paper gives you confidence and focus.

While it is possible to start a business without a written business plan, I strongly recommend you make one, no matter how simple. Even if your idea is to run a dog-washing business after school, plan out the basic ideas on paper. Here is a very simple format you can begin with; it's ideal for small service businesses or one-time ventures:

1. The idea
2. Who will buy it
3. How it will be made or sold
4. When and where you will do it
5. Initial investment required
6. Profit potential.

Here are two fictional examples.

LAKE FLEABEGONE DOGWASH SERVICE

---

1. *The idea*: Flea baths for dogs and cats
2. *Who will buy it*: Neighborhood pet owners in the Lake Fleabegone area
3. *How sold*: Flyers, door-to-door visits, and word of mouth
4. *When and where*: In customers' driveways on weekends and in spare time

5. *Initial Investment*: $520

6. *How much made*: $10 per dog, more for additional services. Could make $150 on a Saturday; more if we hire local kids as help. We expect to make about $2000 during the summer.

Here is a more detailed plan for a college service business.

COLLEGE COMPUMATCH COMPANY

---

1. SERVICE IDEA

   Mitch Macher and Greg Arius will offer a complete on-line "shopping guide" for Gadzoo College students seeking roommates or dates.

2. MARKET

   Gadzoo College has approximately 5,300 students with a freshman class of about 2,050. A survey by student government revealed that 39 percent of freshmen were unhappy with the roommate selected by the University, and 65 percent felt the match had been adequate but not ideal. Our random sampling of 47 students indicated that over half would try out at least one of our service options. A similar service is already operating at Pedigree-Mill University (PU), and is highly successful; none exists yet at Gadzoo.

3. MARKETING AND PROMOTION

   College CompuMatch will be advertised through the *Gadzoo Gazette* and on the campus radio station. We will also make flyers, posters, and send electronic messages to users of Gadzoo's central computer. Word of mouth spreads quickly at Gadzoo.

Our kickoff promotion will sponsor a computer match dance. With the price of a ticket comes a brief questionnaire that we will put on-line. On the night of the dance, ticketholders will be given a list of their ten most compatible people, in rank order, along with a color-coded badge to locate them easily.

4. OPERATIONS

Greg Arius has cleared the first tier of approval with the University to use the central computer.

Dating option: For $10 membership and $8 per user-hour, students will be given a valid password into a user account, on which they can leave their anonymous profile, check other profiles, and send messages to other users.

Roommate option: For $10, users will be matched with other students based on a compatibility questionnaire.

5. FINANCIAL PROJECTIONS

(August 25, 1988, to December 21, 1988)

a. EXPENSES:

Advertising		$ 250
User-hours		$ 480
Other		$ 100
	Total	$ 830

b. INCOME:

Kickoff dance		$ 500
Dating service		$1400
Roommate referral		$ 800
	Total	$2700

We are currently working on a contract with the Admissions Department to take over their current roommate match program. We are confident the deal will come through since the office is understaffed and registers many complaints from freshmen.

We also plan to franchise the software and concept to other universities through the Association of Collegiate Entrepreneurs.

If your business idea is more sophisticated, if you need financing, or if you simply wish to plan in closer detail, design it using the following framework:

1. Service or Product
2. Goals
3. Entrepreneurial team
4. Market
5. Competition
6. Marketing plan
7. Sales strategy
8. Management
9. Operations
10. Bookkeeping
11. Legal
12. Timetable
13. Financial projections
14. Personal purpose (optional yet highly recommended).

Each of these 14 items will be summarized on the following pages and the concepts will be expanded throughout the book. A sample business plan using this format appears at the end of this chapter, and a blank business plan worksheet has been included in Appendix C.

Remember, many of the following details may not apply to you, especially if you are just starting a small service business catering to students. Many entrepreneurs began their businesses by the seat of their pants, not by the tips of their pens. The formalities can come with expansion.

1. Service or Product   Describe in a sentence or a short paragraph what your business will provide. Leave the details for other sections.

2. Goals   Put down your overall financial goal, projecting the dollar amount of business (total sales volume) you would like to do within a certain amount of time, such as one year. Leave the details to be expanded on in Item 13, Financial Projections.

Also list any significant achievements you would like to accomplish within a certain period of time, such as "Complete phase 1 of software development by September 6" or "Give 50 performances by June 1."

3. The entrepreneurial team   Describe the key team members if there are others beside yourself. What role will each person take? What background does each person contribute?

This item is crucial to your success if you will be using the business plan to obtain capital. Several venture capitalists I consulted report that *who* the entrepreneurs are is much more important than the idea itself. A useful booklet, *Raising Venture Capital: An Entrepreneur's Guidebook*, published by the accounting firm of Deloitte, Haskins & Sells, advises entrepreneurs to include résumés of key members. Even if your plan is simple or not targeted at lenders, make sure it addresses how your and/or other team members' talents will be put to work.

4. Market   Pinpoint your buyers. What group characteristics do they have? (Occupation, age, location, buying power, etc.) How big is the market? What motivates people to buy? What prices will you charge? Prove that there is an unfilled need you can fill. Chapter 5 covers these ideas in detail.

Sources say that the market analysis is often the most important item in a business plan. Lenders typically turn to this section immediately after reading the cover letter. Even for informal business plans, knowing your market is the basis for designing the rest of the plan.

5. Competition   Identify your competition by name. Also consider indirect competition. What else is competing for the $5 J. College Student has available for entertainment this week? Define how your product or service is unique in the marketplace, or how it meets buyers' needs better than competitors' products.

Experts say that many entrepreneurs overlook competition in their zeal to begin their new businesses. Give it careful treatment in your plan. It will make your plan seem much more credible to potential investors and it will help you produce a better marketing strategy. For example, when I was designing the proposal for this book, my agent instructed me to include competition analysis.

6. Marketing plan   Describe how you will get your product or service out to the customers. How will it be distributed? (E.g., through wholesalers, retailers, mail order, etc.) How will you advertise? What unique promotions or free publicity can you generate? Chapters 5 and 6 are loaded with creative ideas in these areas.

7. Sales strategy   Map out a sales strategy. Who will do the selling? Yourself, employees, independent salespeople? How will it be done? (Door-to-door, phone, trade shows, or other outlets.) When will sales take place? (E.g., time of year, time of day, etc.) What kind of sales quotas will be expected and how much commission will be paid? How large will an average order be and how many calls will it take to get one order?

Chapter 7 offers tips on sales techniques like prospecting for customers and closing the sale.

8. Management   Outline your organizational structure and management philosophy. What role will each of your partners or employees take? How will they be paid? If you are working alone, how will you organize your time? What organizational procedures will you standardize, and how much will be left flexible? Do you plan to experiment with management innovations such as cooperative ownership, profit sharing, or productivity incentives? (See Chapter 10.)

9. Operations   Describe where and how your business will be run. Will you operate out of your home or dorm room, rent space, or have mobile operations? When will operations take place? What equipment and office supplies will be needed? Will you need a ledger, phone, computer, stationery, stamps, furnishings, etc.? From whom will you order merchandise or raw materials? How will goods be produced? What raw materials and equipment will be necessary? How will you store inventory and equipment? (See Chapters 4 and 8.)

10. Bookkeeping   Describe how you will keep records. Will you use computer software or a ledger book? How will you do your billing? Where will you do your banking and how will you invest profits? Will you enlist the help of an accountant or financial advisor?

11. Legal Identify the requirements you must fulfill to operate a legal business. Do zoning, health department, or campus regulations apply to you? Do you plan to incorporate or obtain a patent or protect copyrights, or trademarks? What licenses, such as a business license, state seller's permit, etc., must you apply for? Which taxes must you file? When must you pay them? (See Chapter 9.)

12. Timetable Make a working timetable. Include achievement milestones, deadlines for key sales goals, and a target date for your grand opening. Also consider when taxes are due and when accounts payable should be paid and accounts receivable collected.

13. Financial projections Estimate your budget. Think realistically and base your numbers on actual research wherever possible. Add up overhead—fixed costs such as rent, equipment, etc.—and figure out variable costs such as commissions, cost of goods, etc. Set a target sales volume based on your overall goal. You can get a rough idea of your profits by subtracting your estimated costs from your estimated sales.

These estimations and calculations actually are simpler than they look, and will be explained with a step-by-step method in the next chapter.

Determine financial needs. How much initial investment is needed? Can earnings from early sales be reinvested? Identify possible sources of funding. Will you use personal funds, or reinvest earnings from early sales into company growth, or will you seek a loan from a bank, or obtain capital by giving investors equity (that is, part ownership in the company)? (See "obtaining startup money" in the next chapter.)

Also consider growth potential. Is your business in an expanding field? How large is the potential market? Do you expect to sell your business or continue it as a career?

Note: Venture capitalists will analyze this section of the business plan *very* closely and structure their deals accordingly. Even if you don't seek financing, or if your enterprise is as simple as washing your neighbors' windows, pay close attention to the bottom line.

14. Personal purpose Put things in perspective. What will you do with the money you make? How will entrepreneurship benefit you in the long run? Why in the world are you doing something that requires much more effort than an ordinary job? What values will you uphold in your business practices?

While writing this part down is not expected by venture capitalists, I strongly recommend that you write it just for you. Having a written statement of values can make decision making easier later, and you've got to know your own purpose and goals intimately in order to inspire the loyalty of potential customers, employees, and other business people.

PUTTING YOUR BUSINESS PLAN TO WORK

The actual business plan you make might be simpler or more complex than the model given, depending on the scope of your business and whether you seek financing. I recommend you start with a simple draft. State the basics, such as what your product or service is, who will buy it, and an estimate of income and expenses. Consider beginning yours using the worksheet in Appendix C at the end of this book.

A well-researched and concisely written business plan can open doors for venture capital. The next chapter will uncover sources of capital and show you how to submit your business plan.

But the business plan is mainly for *you*. Use it as a basis for making decisions, setting goals, and using your time. Unsuccessful people make decisions based on whatever seems least stressful at the moment. Don't follow the path of least resistance—instead, follow your business plan. It will help you stay focused on only those activities that build your business quickly and solidly. Every minute you take to plan could save hours of hassle later.

The complete business plan below goes into considerable depth to show how much planning is possible. Bear in mind that your business idea might not require so much planning.

LAWN GRAPHICS CO.

Jim Toro, President
333 Bowling Green
Grassland, MO 34543

1. SERVICE OR PRODUCT
   Lawn mowing and landscaping with a flair.

2. GOALS
   Sales volume: $11,000 by October 1, 1992.
   Achievements: To have received a contract from Holiday Inn or one of the local hotels to renovate its landscape design; to have three additional employees by June 1.

3. THE ENTREPRENEURIAL TEAM
   Key members: Jim Toro, Dave Snapper, and Tory Lonby.
   Backgrounds and unique strengths: Jim Toro will act as president, and draws on experience in Jim's Services Co. Dave Snapper will take care of public relations, and draws on advertising skills and high personal creativity. Tory Lonby will maintain equipment and manage additional employees.

4. MARKET
   Characteristics of buyers: Corporations and businesses with landscaping needs, hotels, etc. Also wealthy homeowners in Grassland and nearby areas. Our informal market research turned up several companies interested in the concept, and Jim Toro's customers were 100 percent satisfied with the diagonal lawn-mowing pattern.
   Prices we will charge: $150 per month for midsized corporate customers.

5. COMPETITION

   Names of other competitors: Martin's Gardens and Environmental Landscaping Co.

   What they offer and how much the service costs: Standard landscaping, $165 per month for large private homes.

   Indirect competition: Janitors and in-house groundskeepers.

   Success ingredient: Lawns will be mowed in diagonal paths for a professional look. We will offer corporations the option of having their logo mowed into their front lawn by raising mower blades one notch, or we will design logos with ornamental gardening.

6. MARKETING PLAN

   Distributorship: Not applicable.

   Advertising policy: Yellow pages, flyers, insert in local newspaper.

   Promotion opportunities: We will send a press release to the *Grassland Prairie Dog* and other local newspapers, and aim for a spot on "PM Magazine."

7. SALES STRATEGY

   Type of sales force: Jim and Tory in person; Dave on phone followup.

   Selling strategy: Door-to-door with photo album of previous jobs; word of mouth.

   Sales quotas: Goal of 15 corporate customers and 45 homeowners.

   Commissions: Not applicable.

8. MANAGEMENT

   Division of responsibilities: See above.

   Organizational procedures: The three partners will share

the work load and profits equally and will be paid $10 per hour in wages; we will have company meetings Friday afternoons at Bailey's Pub.

Management philosophy and innovations: We will try to create a fun working atmosphere, encourage cooperation, and have a productivity incentive plan.

9. OPERATIONS

Business location: Office at Jim Toro's house, operations throughout Greater Grassland.

Fixture checklist: See operating budget.

Services used: Barter for accounting services.
Barter for sharpening services.

Raw material: Gasoline discount at Lomas Exxon.
Fertilizer, tools, etc., from Discount Hardware Supply Co.

Inventory Suppliers: Not applicable.
Delivery: Not applicable.

Tools and equipment (see operating budget): One truck, one riding mower, one rotary weed chopper, four push mowers with collection bags. Various clippers and pruners. Miscellaneous small tools.

10. BOOKKEEPING

Type of system: Jim Toro will keep records on his home computer.

Billing policy: Once a month, with 30 days allowed for accounts receivable.

Bank and type of accounts: Last National Bank, business checking account and personal savings.

11. LEGAL

(Will be checked by Jim Toro and his sister Rhonda Toro, CPA.)

Business license:
Fictitious Name Business License (DBA): We are in the process of obtaining it.
Seller's permit: Not applicable.
Zoning ordinances: Not applicable.
Liability coverage and bonding: Bonding through Cochina Insurance Co.
Tax schedules: To be checked.

12. TIMETABLE
February 1, 1992:
Begin marketing to discover if there is interest in the logo-mowing idea.
March 1
Purchase office supplies
Clear licenses and legal matters
April 1
Purchase equipment
April 15
Begin landscaping work
April 30
Monthly receipts $2000
June 1
Hire three employees
June 30
Monthly receipts $2500
July 30
Monthly receipts $3500
August 30
Montly receipts $3000
September 30
Monthly receipts $1500

October 1
> Profits divided among partners
> Planning meeting for next year

13. FINANCIAL PROJECTIONS

Summary of operating budget: Total income $11,500 from total sales and services and interest on savings.

Amount of startup capital needed: $3350 for equipment and cash reserve. We plan to raise this amount from personal savings. We also have a line of credit from Discount Hardware Supply.

Growth potential: If the idea catches on, we may open Lawn Graphics Companies in other cities.

Future financial plans: Will invest profits in high-interest savings certificates at Last National Bank.

14. PERSONAL PURPOSE

Personal sacrifices, benefits, and work values: Our goal is a profitable season, and the start of a new trend in the landscaping industry.

4
CAPITALIZING ON A SHOESTRING How to Find Those Hidden Resources

"Entrepreneuring successfully is achieving
wealth by providing solutions to people's
problems and thereby creating employment,
stimulating innovation, and reinvesting
wealth in the dreams of others."
—A. David Silver,
The Silver Prescription

BECOMING AN ENTREPRENOIR

featuring
Beth Whiting of All Beth's Creations

Many students waste their lives watching the one-eyed hypnotist, but one particular student has been on the other side of the TV screen—twice. Many students would like to be able to put themselves through college. This one can. And many students wish they could set their own hours, do something creative, and make good money. This one does.

Beth Whiting, a self-confident yet modest graduate of Country Day High School in Cincinnati, Ohio, achieved these things through her business, All Beth's Creations. One day when she was 12, she painted some hair ribbons to amuse herself. Later she brought them to a local children's clothing store. The owner took a liking to her and agreed to display the ribbons. They sold quickly. Before long, Beth was filling orders for 20 stores in 12 states, including a department store and a small retail chain. As business sped up, All Beth's Creations took in $20,000 in two years.

Considering that few teenagers are raking in big dollars and paying taxes at 13, the media became very interested in Miss Whiting. She was featured in *Seventeen* magazine, *Entrepreneur* magazine, and several newspapers. Then she appeared on "The Phil Donahue Show" in 1983 and soon after on the "Today" show.

A national celebrity? Not from Beth's viewpoint. She considers her work just an "extensive hobby" and has managed to convince her friends it is, too. Even though everybody at school has seen and read about Beth Whiting, *entrepreneur*, they generally know and accept her as Beth Whiting, *person*. Since she works only an average of ten hours a week, she has time to study, compete on the soccer and track teams, and go cross-country skiing or shopping with friends.

Financial independence, the classic American Dream, is hers already. College expenses are well under control, since the University of Southern California offered her a scholarship worth $40,000.

To earn a degree in the Real World, one must take some courses from life's School of Hard Knocks. One time, Beth ordered 96,000 wooden beads from Germany, expecting to mass-produce beaded hair barrettes. Soon after, the barrettes went out of style. She is still trying to come up with a creative use for the 80,000 beads she still has rolling around in her basement!

Characteristically, Beth considers it just a minor setback. She channeled her energy into hand-painted T-shirts, men's ties, and casual cotton dresses. Like many precocious entrepreneurs, Beth's biggest initial obstacle was overcoming the age barrier. She says, "At first I had a few problems with people wondering if this was just some little girl selling a couple of ribbons to make a little extra money. But as I expanded my line and became more professional, people saw I wasn't joking around."

Apple Computer Corp., now a billion-dollar industry, owes its beginnings to a couple of young entrepreneurs who tinkered with electronics in a garage. Steve Jobs and his partner, Steve Wozniak, were barely out of their teens when they conceived of the idea of building a computer that ordinary people could afford. To fund their dream they sold their one worldly possession, a van, for about $2,000. From miscellaneous electronic paraphernalia and a spark of entrepreneurial inspiration, they built their first prototype, the Apple I.

Entrepreneurs are notorious for unglamorous business startups. Kim Merritt of Kim's Khocolate started in a church kitchen. Beth Whiting of All Beth's Creations began with a couple of hair ribbons. Ken Appel of KB Books got his start selling books out of the back of his car. When I started Van's Services in high school, all I had was a rake and a lawn mower. You don't necessarily have to have a lot of money to start a business, just a willingness to improvise. What you've got in your head can make up for whatever you don't happen to have in your wallet.

YOUR INITIAL OPERATING BUDGET

The initial operating budget doesn't need to be complicated, nor do you need a crystal ball to predict every single expense and sale in the future. The reason for having a budget is to give you an idea of how much capital you'll need at the start.

In order to know how much startup capital you'll require, you first need to know what items it will take to get started, such as tools, raw materials, etc. Make a written "shopping list" of items and services you'll need. Check around to get an idea of prices. Total it up, *then double it.* Experienced entrepreneurs say they always overlooked hidden costs that seemed to pop up from everywhere during the startup phase.

I strongly recommend that you have access to a cash reserve in addition to the money budgeted for specific known costs. These expenses should be justified by a realistic appraisal of projected income. Estimate the business income for a certain period of time, according to your sales goals.

Here is an example continued from Lake Fleabegone.

DOGWASH SERVICE

PROJECTED EXPENDITURES	
Flea shampoo (two gallons)	$ 32.00
Rubber gloves (two pairs)	5.00
Hose and nozzle	18.00
Metal tub	23.00
Assorted brushes, etc.	12.00
Advertising flyers (1000)	40.00
Other, including cash reserve	130.00
Total Cost	$ 260.00
Now double it	$ 520.00
PROJECTED INCOME	
May to September	$2500.00
PROJECTED PROFIT	$1980.00

FINDING STARTUP MONEY

Most people assume you have to be rich to start a business, but this particular bit of miseducation has killed countless ideas. Don't buy this fatalistic hogwash. There are dozens of alternatives for the resourceful individual.

Shoestringing   One alternative is "shoestringing" it. Shoestringing is the art of starting a business with almost no equipment, resources, or capital. The term "starting on a shoestring" probably comes from this old fable my Dad passed on to me:

> Once upon a time in a medieval burg far, far away, a certain young shoemaker's apprentice only had enough leather to make a few shoestrings. He traded them with a tanner for a larger piece of leather, from which he made a pair of shoes. When he sold them, he had enough

"I'm afraid you're barking up the wrong tree."

money to buy leather to make two more pairs. Two
led to four and four to eight. . . . He ended up building
the biggest shoe shop in the entire city!

Shoestringing can be especially useful in a service business. Because you are paid by the job and don't need expensive inventory or manufacturing operations, you can
get started with almost no cash. Whatever equipment you
do need, you might be able to obtain in resourceful ways.
In my small window-washing business, I got a number of
items on a barter exchange. My squeegee and a couple of
minutes of work were my best credit card! In fact, bartering—the age-old practice of exchanging goods and services directly without using money—is making a modern
comeback. Many young entrepreneurs use bartering to get
vital goods and services by simply trading their own goods
and services. Today many trading networks are springing
up all over the country to accommodate large-quantity
trades or complex trades involving more than two parties.

Moonlighting   Another alternative is moonlighting, where
you could take a part-time job for income or training while
you're getting your enterprises going. Professional speaker
Laurie Stewart worked for another speaker and entertainer
Jim Hall worked in a grocery store while they were developing their performance routines.

Phasing   Phasing, a similar alternative, involves financing
your big entrepreneurial dream in progressive phases, using
smaller yet surer enterprises. For example, I mowed lawns,
tutored, and washed windows only to plow the money back
into expenses related to writing my books. Not only does
this approach yield money faster than a part-time job, the
entrepreneurial experience proves invaluable later on.

Moreover, if you decide to seek outside financing, nothing looks better to a venture capitalist than proof of entrepreneurial ability.

OPM   The last alternative is a secret called "OPM." OPM isn't a drug made from poppies; the closest thing to an OPM den is a bank. OPM stands for "Other People's Money." OPM sources include:

1. *Family and acquaintances.* If you believe in what you're doing strongly enough, those around you are likely to believe in you, too. Karl Edelmann's father believed so strongly in his kids he helped them set up a competitive auto parts factory.

In approaching your parents or a rich uncle, keep in mind they may be even more difficult to persuade than a banker; after all, they've seen not only your successes but your failures, too. Therefore, make a well-crafted written business plan that contains specific dollar amounts and target dates so you can convince them your efforts will be worth supporting.

2. *Campus Entrepreneurs' Clubs.* Many of the larger entrepreneurs' clubs and ACE affiliates have special funds set aside for members.

3. *Private lenders.* After a highly successful beginning, Dan Bienenfeld's company, Design Look, Inc., was ready for expansion. He and his partner wrote down the name of every millionaire they knew. With a proven track record and an 80-page business plan, they were able to raise $80,000. Private parties are more likely to lend young entrepreneurs money than a bank or a venture capitalist, as long as you either cut them in for a share of the company (equity) or borrow the money at a high interest rate.

4. *Bankers and venture capitalists.* Institutional lenders tend to be very cautious about dealing with inexperienced entrepreneurs. However, sometimes they will bet on a good risk. For example, Kim Merritt got a $75,000 loan from a Maryland bank. In this case, they weren't trusting an 18-year-old, they were trusting an entrepreneur with seven years' experience! (The fact that her parents cosigned for the loan didn't hurt either.)

OBTAINING A LOAN

"The key to getting money," says venture capitalist Buzz Woolley, "is catching the attention of people like me who can write a check. Entrepreneurs' business plans have got to convince me that they know what they're doing and that it's a good idea."

A concise and carefully researched business plan is absolutely necessary for obtaining a major loan. The plan itself could be anywhere from 10 to 100 or more pages, depending on the complexity. Introducing it should be a brief cover letter explaining who you are and what your objective is. That is followed by an "executive summary," a one- to three-page summary of your product or service, management team, market, and projected financial data. Be sure to highlight the "success ingredient" that puts you ahead of the competition.

Before submitting the documents, find a fellow entrepreneur who knows a venture capitalist and have him or her recommend your idea. If you are granted an interview, demonstrate hot enthusiasm but keep a cool head for facts and negotiation. Since negotiating is complex, talk to as many experienced entrepreneurs and bankers as you can before even considering a loan, and since getting a loan in the first place is a serious undertaking, read all you can. A good concise introductory guide is *Raising Venture Capital: An Entrepreneur's Guidebook*, published by Deloitte, Haskins & Sells. (See Appendix A for other resources.)

LOCATION

Almost all student entrepreneurs operate out of their homes and personal vehicles. It costs nothing extra and these locations create legal tax deductions. However, in deciding where to work, consider not only cost but your potential productivity. Can you work with your little brother running up and down the hall? Are you willing to explain to every visitor to your dorm room why half of it is taken up with boxes of inventory?

BUYING EQUIPMENT, SERVICES, AND SUPPLIES

Equipment In buying your equipment, smart wheeling and dealing could save you a wad of green.

Barter whenever possible.

Spend money ONLY on what is absolutely necessary.

First priority should go to those things that return money right away, like tools or inventory. As the owner, every penny for a "business expense" is a penny out of your profits, so save the gold-plated paper clips and limo service till you're in the 50 percent tax bracket.

1. *Buy used equipment.* Although the image and reliability of new equipment is often worth it, used equipment that has been well-maintained can keep startup costs low.

2. *Family tools are sacred.* If you borrow something, treat it as if it were the property of the Royal Family. (In

a sense, it is.) When Tom Mangee, a teenage entrepreneur I knew in Kalamazoo, Michigan, started sealing driveways, he would slide several buckets full of oozing, foul-smelling tar into the back of the family station wagon. It made his parents just a little nervous. Later he bought a used truck. Mr. and Mrs. Mangee breathed much easier.

3. *Practice regular maintenance.* Marc Magor, who teaches hang gliding, cautions, "Safe equipment is 100 percent necessary in my business. There can't be any indication of wear and tear."

Services Try to keep costs low when buying such services as photocopying, a post office box, long distance phone services, etc. Typical supplies for student-run business could include business cards, stationery, and desk supplies. Personal computers or user privileges on the school computer are becoming more common for even the least sophisticated businesses.

Supplies If you are running a manufacturing or retail outfit, your profits and company reputations will be dramatically affected by the price and quality of merchandise or raw materials you buy. Your cash flow may also be affected by your suppliers' policies. Sound *cents* must be exercised when selecting and dealing with suppliers.

A positive note: Your state seller's permit (discussed in Chapter 9) entitles you to buy wholesale goods for resale without paying state sales tax.

1. *Buy only from reputable suppliers and business services.* Shop around. Order catalogs. Check who your competition uses as suppliers. Ken Appel had some bad experiences:

"One of the big publishers sent us the same order *three times*. We had to send the shipment back. They're still sending us bills!"

2. *Buy on credit, if the terms are right.* Ken Appel's book store carries an inventory worth as much as a small house. He was careful to find publishers who would extend as much as 60 days' credit. That way, only a little up-front money was needed.

3. *Buy only as much as you need.* Beth Whiting imported 96,000 wooden beads from Germany only to have them go out of style. Market testing, gut feelings, advice from other entrepreneurs, and experience are the best yardsticks for buying.

4. *Order long before you run out.* Having an inventory of 400 of my own books, I thought I'd *never* run out. When I did, I couldn't fill an important customer's order for weeks.

5. *Maintain trust.* One bad check or delayed payment, and your suppliers could cut you off, stereotyping you as "just another unreliable kid." Prove them wrong—for the sake of all of us.

SURVIVING STARTUP

Know what it's like to work so hard you forget what it's like to be normal? You will, after the first few weeks of business. At first it may seem like you are digging the Panama Canal—all by yourself. Suddenly, picking blueberries for two bucks an hour doesn't seem so bad after all . . .

There will be millions of tasks to do as you put your business plan into action: licenses to get, bookkeeping systems to set up, flyers to print, business cards to buy, customers to find and serve, and, hopefully, money to deposit in your bank account.

It will be tempting to try to accomplish every item on your list at once, but since you are smarter than that, make a plan and work it.

Frustrations and setbacks are part of the history of every successful entrepreneur who ever lived. But permanent quitting isn't. Hang in there! Remember your big dream. Laurie Stewart believes, "Obstacles are what we see when we take our eyes off the goal."

Most problems can be foreseen. Others can't. Kim Merritt's story symbolizes the true initiation rites into entrepreneurhood:

> "I was pretty green, just age 11, and I was trying to move 200 pounds of candy at Heritage Days county craft fair. But it was 95 degrees in the shade, and all anybody wanted in the world was snow cones—and that booth was right in front of mine.
>
> Well, the chocolate was a mess. We brought it home and sat it in the living room. We just looked at it for two weeks. One night Dad decided he was getting sick of tripping over it and was going to throw it out. At that point I wasn't very interested in business and agreed to call it quits.
>
> That night I got a call from Rhonda Garlitz, a local merchant. She said she had tried my candy and wanted to sell it. Mom and I decided to melt down our chocolate and try again.
>
> That started my business all over again, and from that point on I started selling in stores and at school."

If it weren't for Kim's luck and determination, her business would have died of sunstroke. For startup, the best preventive medicine your business can have is cash flow, which is best achieved by swiftly attracting customers. The next three chapters can help you locate, attract, and gain their patronage.

5

USE A RIFLE, NOT A SHOTGUN

Finding All the Customers You Can Handle

"If you want to catch a mouse,
think like a cheese."
—Dr. Melanie Brown,
Attaining Personal Greatness

GETTING RICH

featuring
Kim Merritt of Kim's Khocolate, Inc.

When Kim Merritt toured Switzerland to learn the art of making chocolate, it was not merely a sightseeing tour. It was a business trip, financed by her growing business, Kim's Khocolate. Then again, it wasn't exactly a typical business trip either—for liability purposes, the then 17-year-old businesswoman first had to secure her parents' permission!

Kim's Khocolate owes its beginnings to Kim's grandmother, who gave the curious 11-year-old a chocolate-making kit. It only took one batch and she was hooked. That year she launched Kim's Khocolate and began selling chocolate at school and church bazaars.

Kim's Khocolate is a thriving business operating near Cumberland, Maryland. Now 20, Kim has opened a chocolate factory with a $75,000 loan. It has several employees and equipment to make chocolate and fudge wholesale. It was a big step up from making chocolate at home and in her church kitchen.

One of Kim's earliest successes was a fund-raising promotion at her high school that netted the company nearly $9,000. In 38 days, she and the

36 hired students made 19,100 candy bars. She remembers, "In the course of making so much chocolate, there was not much time to study. My grades fell way off."

Today Kim is involved in major corporate contracts such as A&P supermarkets and Apple Computer. She says, "Apple gave me a reject dead mouse and we made a mold over it." (Both the mouse and the mold are of the manufactured kind, not the reproducing kind!)

Kim's knack for marketing and promoting herself has made her one of the most well-known student entrepreneurs in the nation. Her face has been seen in *People* magazine, *Newsweek on Campus*, *Seventeen*, *Career World*, and *Glamour*; and she has been featured on "PM Magazine" and her local TV station. She also was featured in *Playboy*—for her chocolate, of course.

In her home town and school, Kim is famous. Her red Nissan 300 ZX sports a personalized license plate, CHOCLIT, and she sponsors a youth recreation team. With all the publicity they've had, the team is sweet on her. The chocolate treats she serves up don't hurt either.

Kim owes part of her success to encouragement from her parents and other entrepreneurs. Kim claims, "I wouldn't be in business if it weren't for my mother." Mrs. Merritt responds, "A young entrepreneur is the most exciting thing this country has ever produced. I think teachers should be trained to spot these kids early and encourage them."

Most of all, Kim's success comes from believing

in herself. She asserts, "I've never been one to be bashful." Her spirit is mirrored by a poster she has in her chocolate shop: "To be good is not enough when you dream of being great." Her advice to other aspiring entrepreneurs is, "Listen to everybody. Take the good things and the bad things and put them together. Listen to your intuition and then do what you feel is right."

Doug Melinger and David Goldsmith made a big booboo. The two opportunity-seekers from Syracuse University in New York had speculated that they could make a big profit by selling boxer shorts to sunworshipping college students on their springtime pilgrimage to Fort Lauderdale, but it didn't turn out that way. David narrates:

"We got down to the strip in record time. After all, we figured we were going to be millionaires in two days. The first day we tried selling them along the strip, but that didn't work. Then we decided to go into hotels to sell, but the security guards hampered us. Then we started to go to the beach and we were asking girls with bikinis, with no money or anything, if they'd like to buy these shorts. That didn't work.

After three days, we hadn't even sold a pair. I mean, even our friends wouldn't buy them. At that point, we were nervous wrecks. I think we were the only two guys in history to go to Fort Lauderdale and not go in the ocean, not go in a bar, not pick up a woman. When we ate out, he would have the hamburger and I would have the fries."

Marketing, from a student entrepreneur's perspective, involves defining and refining: defining exactly who your customers are and refining the product or service in order to meet customer needs.

DEFINING YOUR MARKET

A good way to start is to sit down and make a list of every type of person you think might buy your product or service. The more specific you can get, the easier it will be to choose prices, prepare packaging or advertising, and hone your selling approach. Make a customer profile, beginning with the following questions:

1. What age groups do your customers come from? (Teenagers? College-age adults? Career-age and middle-age adults? Senior citizens?)

2. What are their occupations and income bracket? (Professionals? Teachers? Students? Homemakers?)

3. Will males or females make the larger percentage of sales?

4. How much money do they spend on services like yours? What media sources are they influenced by? (MTV? The *Wall Street Journal*? The campus newspaper or radio?)

5. Where are they located?

And, specifically for the campus market,

6. What campus subgroups can you cater to? (Fraternities and sororities? Athletes? Yuppies? Intellectuals?)

7. Will you try to target commuter students? Apartment residents? Graduate students? Dormies?

"Miss Allen, please bring me a small Bavarian cap and a flute."

8. Where and how do your prospects spend their free time?

The answers/guesses to these questions will help you prepare initial promotion and sales strategies. Experience will modify them. Once you actually start doing business, you invariably will discover new markets, as well as finding out which ones from your original list are the most consistent buyers.

CO-EVOLVING WITH YOUR COMPETITORS

Student entrepreneurs frequently get their ideas when they see someone else doing it first. They go and do it better.

Software creator David Fogel noticed that the market

was in need of a good text adventure (an on-line "book" where *you* decide what happens next). He saw that Infocom, the giant in the field, was doing only a halfway job. David came up with "Holmes," an adaptation of Sir Conan Doyle's classic work.

Competition is not usually as big a concern for student entrepreneurs as it is for full-scale businesses. Student-run enterprises are either so innovative no one else is doing them, or small enough to survive by serving the customers who "fall between the cracks" of larger businesses.

Competition is normal and natural; it's a sign that there is money to be made. All you need to do to survive and even thrive is find a creative way to do it better, faster, or cheaper than the other guys.

PRICING AND PACKAGING

Ken Appel is an easy-going guy—especially over a Bud Light. Ask any of the customers at KB Books and they'll agree. But the real reason they buy from him is that his prices are so low he almost pays them to buy. Price is one reason student entrepreneurs manage to get a piece of the market. They can usually undercut the competition because of their low overhead or operating costs.

Probably the simplest way to choose a price is to rely on your competition. Take their price, lower it slightly, and deliver better service. Then see if it turns a good profit for you. Simple. At KB Books, they did just that. They charged less than list price for textbooks, not 6 percent more, like the university bookstore did.

If you want to get more sophisticated, you could consult some practical small business books for pricing formulas. Stores generally mark up items 30 to 100 percent over cost. One source suggests counting up your cost per job or per product (taking into consideration operating costs like rent, office supplies, etc.) and adding it to what you feel a fair hourly price would be. The higher your skill, the more you can charge. Scott Mize's fee for computer software consulting has run as high as $60 per hour.

Always charge what your product or service is worth. If people really need something, they will pay the going rate. The best bet for profits is not constant hype, but a satisfied list of customers who will give you repeat business.

Product packaging Chocolate, the consuming passion, causes otherwise rational, stoic persons to hedonistically heed its siren call—lust at first sight. Consequently, it's not surprising that Kim Merritt uses attractive gold labels on clear plastic wrappers to help the buyer's eyes convince the buyer's brain that the buyer's tongue will be in ecstasy.

If you have an item you want to sell door-to-door, retail, or on consignment, make sure it grabs the shopper's attention long enough to check it out. Colors, bold print, metallic foil, and clear plastic are good materials. A simple red ribbon around a wooden spoon at a Christmas craft booth doubles its appeal.

Service packaging With a product, you dress it up and let it sell itself. With a service, *you* are the package. From the first impression to the completion of your job, your image will shape your customer's attitude about doing business with you. Items like your brochures, business cards, advertising, the car you drive, and the clothes you wear all have a strong influence—much of it subconscious.

The most important part of your image is the way you do business. Frankly, flaky folks fail fast. A respectable (and ultimately profitable) image is built out of being on time, answering letters and phone calls right away, and backing up any product defects or gaps in your service.

TEST MARKETING

Remember the Edsel? Ford's fiasco could have been avoided if it had bothered to find out whether potential buyers would purchase such a car. Check the market pulse before you invest a lot of time and money in your product or service. Ask friends, other student entrepreneurs, instructors and mentors, neighbors and family, and especially people from the groups you target as potential buyers. Be specific about what you will do and what you will charge, then gauge the response. Big ears do a lot better at this point than a big mouth. (Save your breath for publicity, covered in the next chapter.)

Some students have gone so far as to knock on every door in a dormitory to get a feel for whether people are interested in their product or service. If you do this, I suggest you make a special effort to leave a very positive feeling with the people you meet. Leave them a free sample, or perhaps a cookie for their time.

In fact, free samples are the best form of advertising because they let the product speak for itself. I feel they are also the least damaging to a society's sanity. Would you rather Happy-Brite Bubbles Soap Co. send you a packet of detergent in the mail, or bludgeon the whole family's intelligence with a commercial that's supposedly a "hidden camera interview"?

Free samples aren't just restricted to candy and Happy-Brite Bubbles. Why not try something *really* creative? A printed patch of cloth to promote a T-shirt, an excerpt to promote a book or magazine, a video- or audiotape to promote a seminar, a plastic bag containing leaves or grass clippings to say "This is what I could do for your lawn." Paul Cohen, a cofounder of ACE at UCSD, set up his invention patterned after the drinking game "quarters" at one of our fund-raisers. The students loved it so much, we made almost as much money from people trying to bounce quarters through the basketball hoop as we did from selling soda!

Public gatherings and mega-events are ideal for test marketing. These could include:

Malls

Fairs, bazaars, and outdoor festivals

Races (10 Ks, raft races, dogsled trials, etc.)

Parades

The main quad or walkway on campus

Football games and other sports events.

Some events or locations will require permits, so check it out first.

ALTERNATIVE MARKETING STRATEGIES

Preemptive service marketing This is so unconventional that I'll take complete blame for discovering it. When I was running Van's Service, I started the mowing season with a shortage of customers and an abundance of energy. When I saw a lawn I really wanted on my route, I just went ahead and mowed it. Then I knocked on the door with a big smile on my face, and said,

> Your lawn is done,
> Do you like what you see?
> To show I'd like to work for you,
> Today I did it free.

Most of the time, people were delighted once they learned I was sincere. Many hired me on the spot. But I will admit that some Philistines didn't appreciate my work, nor my doggerel rhyme. One snarling ingrate chased me out of the yard, lawn mower and all.

Only a *true* entrepreneur (or a hungry one) would ever try preemptive marketing. It is radically unconventional. It can open doors that had been firmly shut, but I beg you to *think* about the circumstances and outcomes, positive and negative, before you try something like this.

If you're somewhat less nervy about getting your product before the public eye, consider the following:

Selling on consignment   Instead of buying your merchandise outright, some stores will agree to display your goods. When an item sells, the store keeps a percentage; 20 to 50 percent is common. I found consignment sales to be the best way to get local bookstores to sell my first book. University bookstores can be ideal for college entrepreneurs with any kind of T-shirt or novelty item.

Mail order   Put a visually appealing ad in a carefully selected magazine read by potential customers. Then sit back and let the money pour in. (Hint: Run a pilot ad in one magazine before doing several magazines at once.)

Computer shopping   Networks such as The Source, CompuServe, and Dow Jones News/Retrieval are the wave of the future. Though promoting products in these outlets is more expensive than most student entrepreneurs can afford, the smaller computer-based bulletin boards (CBBBs) are within range. Some are even free; for example, the ACE Electronic Network is ideal for advertising and bartering on-line.

People-to-people marketing   Many people still would rather trust a human than a computer. Talk to as many people as you can about your new business, especially at first. Friends and neighbors are a logical starting place. In most cases, they'll be excited to hear what you are doing and will give you valuable advice, contacts, and leads. But remember to put relationships first and profits second. Friendships can be soured if people feel they are being called only as a sales prospect, not as a friend. One nonthreatening avenue is to ask them for advice. I did this when I started a small window washing service. Some conversations went like this:

"Hi, Channing. This is Van. I was wondering if you could give me some advice."

"Sure."

"Well, a friend and I are starting a window washing service, and we're deadlocked over what to call it—The Squeaky Squeegee or Vindow Vipers. What do you think?"

"I like the first one. By the way, how much do you charge?"

"I can drop by and give an estimate. Is today good or is tomorrow better for you?"

Active marketing is necessary to get a company going, but once in a great while customers will drop on you out of the blue. One hot July afternoon, my lawn mowing partner and I were working on a lawn by a busy street. As always, we were sprinting behind the lawn mowers, grass and sweat flying everywhere. Suddenly a brown Datsun 280–Z screeched to a halt right by the curb. A man leaped out of the car and made a beeline for me. I didn't know whether to run or to defend myself with my grass clippers.

For all I knew, this guy could have been some government bureaucrat ready to fine me for running too fast behind a lawn mower. Instead, he pumped my hand and said, "Look, I don't know who you guys are, but I've never seen any two guys work as hard as you. Why don't you come work for me?" Dr. Larry Poel gave Bill and me $200 to landscape his backyard that weekend.

Marketing is like a sociology course; you'll need to make precise distinctions between groups of people. Find the characteristics common to those who buy compared to those who don't. A valuable tip I learned that could save you a lot of effort: Ask new customers how they heard about you. Unless you are so good you could sell a Ford Pinto to Lee Iacocca, sell "Monopoly" games to the Kremlin, or install a Pepsi machine in a Coca Cola plant, you need to give careful thought to who will buy what.

6

WHEN IT PAYS TO BE OFF THE WALL

Advertising, Promotions, and Publicity

"Every adversity, every failure, and every heartache
carries with it the seed of an equivalent or a
greater benefit."
—Napoleon Hill,
Think and Grow Rich

CLOWNING AROUND

featuring
Jim Hall, Professional Entertainer

Five-year-olds love Jemmo the Clown. So do parents and everybody else who experiences his energetic, zany performances. He juggles, rides a unicycle, does tricks, and makes balloon animals at children's parties, corporate picnics, and restaurants. He also has entertained at outdoor fairs and festivals, shopping malls, and children's hospitals.

Jim Hall, who created the character Jemmo when he was in ninth grade, insists that the job involves a lot more than clowning around: "I'm not a circus clown, I'm a professional entertainer. I give a high-energy, unique performance that people will remember. It takes being relaxed and thinking on your feet."

Now a 24-year-old alumnus of the Unversity of California, San Diego, Jim Hall does over 400 performances a year. He says, "Every weekend from age 14 to 24 I've been up in front of people. I went through puberty in a clown suit."

Weekends are prime time for professional entertaining, and Jim will spend as much as 10 or 15 hours a week performing. His fee, $75 for a 60-minute show, represents just a fraction of the time he spends preparing. "My performance time couldn't hold a candle to the time I spend on the phone," he says, and "I also spend a lot of time in solitude, practicing routines and thinking of new ideas."

While the business income runs from $200 to $600 a week, Jim reinvests most of it in advertising costs, which run $525 or more a month. "I'm taking a chance," he says. "I may not even be in business next year. But I find the more I advertise, the more work it puts in my hands. The more I work, the better I feel in front of a group.

"You can't be in this profession for the money," he says. "What I'm doing is investing in 'nonspecific capital' I could carry into any area. This includes things like learning to memorize the kids' names at a party or making another balloon animal for a kid who is crying because his just popped." Jim concludes, "By standing on my principles, my profits will be assured."

The players run out onto the court in front of cheering, hungry fans. Their brown jerseys emblazoned with "Kim's Khocolate" give her chocolate business some of the best advertising possible, and help make Kim Merritt the sweetheart of her community. Her promotion schemes exemplify the creative advertising schemes student entrepreneurs dream up to attract attention.

But more than just getting attention, advertising must have *pull*; that is, positive attraction. If a salesperson switched on a flashlight in my face, he'd probably get my attention all right. He'd also get cracked in the jaw. On the other hand, if he handed me his laminated business card sitting on top of a bowl of Häagen-Dazs ice cream it would be quite a different story.

The best kind of advertising excites people's eyes, ears, tastes, and especially emotions.

When advertising anything, remember three rules:

Wake 'em up: Get their attention. Use strong colors, bold print, and sharp graphics.

Take 'em up: Draw in their attention. What turns them on? Why should they buy?

Shake 'em up: Stir them to action. Tell them who, where, and how much.

Each of these applies to five basic areas of advertising: Printed items, paid advertising, publicity, promotions, and word of mouth.

PRINTED SALES TOOLS

Business cards   Since person-to-person contacts are the most important source of advertising, a business card can turn a handshake into a lasting business contact. Make it simple and appealing. Extra information should go in a brochure, not a business card. The new photo business cards are particularly effective because they keep your name and face permanently linked.

Logo   Designing a logo concept can be almost as fun as naming your business, and it will make your advertising stand out. Since commercial artwork is expensive, use your contacts at school to find a peer to do the fine graphic work. Make it bold and symbolic.

Flyers or brochures   A flyer should knock people out of their shoes. When they've regained consciousness, they should be able to get to the relevant information quickly. Use photos or cartoons—they add life. The Apple Macintosh computer has revolutionized flyer-making and you should have no problem locating a friend with one.

Direct mail This is one of the hottest current marketing trends. However, its success depends directly on having a very appealing ad that will gain the attention of a well-defined market. Note that some on-campus mail does not require stamps and can be cost-effective.

T-shirts, caps, etc. Why not be a walking advertisement? At $5 to $10, a custom T-shirt is one of the best ad values possible. Wear it around school—it may become your favorite piece of clothing. My most prized possession is a sweater with my logo knitted into it. Thanks, Mom.

PAID ADVERTISING

Newspapers Unless ads are cheap or the product is just right, local town newspapers are a bust for student entrepreneurs. However, campus newspapers are often aimed precisely at the market you need to reach. Off-the-wall ads are the most memorable. Brett Kingstone says he saw an ad that said, "FREE SEX!!! (And now that we've got your attention . . .)"

Yellow pages Also a lemon. You'd have to be bananas to pay $100 to $500 a month for such yellow journalism. However, in some businesses, like Jim Hall's "Jemmo" show and Marc Magor's "High Adventure Sports," the ad generates enough calls to pay the bills, most of the time.

In general, avoid paid advertising wherever possible. There are just too many better opportunities for resourceful minds.

50¢

DAILY TIMES

HUNDREDS OF NEWSPAPER
BOXES JAMMED AROUND CITY!

CALLAHAN

PUBLICITY (FREE ADVERTISING!)

You're a wanted man. (Or woman!) The media is dying to interview young entrepreneurs because they are living, breathing human interest stories. A story on a teenage businessperson is a great breather from the latest plane crash or assassination. Since the media wants you, cash in!

Publicity can make student businesses spread like wildfire. After Beth Whiting appeared on the Phil Donahue show to talk about her jewelry business, she began to get orders from all over the U.S. David Fogel got a product review in Apple's *inCider* magazine that drew over 80 responses. Exposure in one source could also land you in another.

The term "PR" doesn't always mean public relations or even PRomotion. It really boils down to Press Release.

It is your first step to getting in magazines, newspapers, or on TV shows. Catching the media's attention before you're known will require breaking the ice first, so your release has got to be sizzling hot, believe me—this is part of my current profession.

A press release can be as short as two or three paragraphs or as long as a couple of pages. Highlight whatever makes you and your business unique. Tell about how you got started and what obstacles you had to overcome. Be sure to include such data as age and where you go to school.

To make a "press kit" that really makes an impression, enclose a press release, a cover letter, a sharp 8 × 10 glossy black and white photo, and copies of other articles that already have been done about you. Having a professional-looking press kit helped Kim Merritt get in *People* magazine and also helped David Fogel get in *USA Today*.

Before you send anything, contact the appropriate person and see if he or she is interested. Later, make a followup call to assure action. Never, ever, ever write a "To whom it may concern" letter. They are fed to paper shredders.

PROMOTIONS

Stage a public event. This is relatively easy on campus. If you are planning to open a pizza-making service, for example, get permission to set up a booth on the quad or sponsor a party for the Greeks. Put up banners, have special napkins, and make sure people have an outrageous time.

Sponsor an entrepreneurs' networking party. Invite campus or community entrepreneurs to exchange business cards and ideas over drinks. One ACE member has a sophisticated networking session at a fancy hotel at least once a month. He charges over $10 a head and pays nothing for the room, since the hotel makes a killing off the drinks. He regularly makes several thousand dollars profit a night.

Teach a class or give a speech. To promote my books, I've put on dozens of free speeches and classes, along with paid seminars. Even if you don't have something to sell, you can build good will in the community and make valuable contacts.

Sponsor a team or perform a conspicuous charity. Unlike cynical pessimists, I believe charitable business promotions are not necessarily self-serving; rather, they give life to events like "USA for Africa" and "Hands across America." Consider, however, that blatant self-interest and short-term gain motives will be transparent. Honey-toned homilies to Lady Liberty, Motherhood, Apple Pie, and Slick Joe's Used Auto Deals smell real bad.

WORD-OF-MOUTH ADVERTISING NETWORKS

Cartoon characters Snuffy Smith and Eliveny gossiping over the fence represent the oldest—and best—source of advertising. The two women are really one WOMAN: a Word-Of-Mouth Advertising Network. Word of mouth works like the old shampoo advertisement: Someone gets a great bargain, and she tells two friends, and *they* tell two friends, and *they* tell . . .

The 200-squared rule And instead of two friends, there could be far more. How many friends, relatives, or acquaintances do you have? Probably more than 200. They, in turn, also have over 200 friends. Now suppose that you needed something, or had something to offer. Through your friends and contacts, you could reach 40,000 people. And through *their* friends, you could reach 8,000,000.

Such numbers seem fantastic, but even if 5 percent of the people at any level were motivated to cooperate, you could reach 100 to 1,000 persons easily. And consider the advantage of networking with other entrepreneurs. We typically know more people who are motivated to buy and sell. I have a whole drawerful of business cards from people I have met through networking, and I have contacts with well over 1,000 more through the Association of Collegiate Entrepreneurs.

What would happen if you could accelerate the whole "tell two friends" process? You can. Offer customers an *incentive* to talk it up. For every new customer they send you, offer them a discount on their next purchase. A hair salon near my house called Shear Images gave me $6 for every new customer I brought them. I passed out their business cards as liberally as my own! Remember one thing, however: Such a system succeeds only if there is really something to hoot and holler about in the first place. Sixteen-year-old Ken Carter, whose catering company has brought in over $30,000 since he started it at age 12, believes, "Word of mouth is about the best advertising there is because all the *good* things you've done get said about you."

30 CREATIVE ADVERTISING IDEAS

1. *Write notices on lecture hall blackboards.* You can reach thousands of students before the janitors erase your message. Get permission first.

2. *Get a spot in school announcements or write an article for the school newspaper.*

3. *Make a business sign.* Jim Hall puts one up while he performs as a clown.

4. *Offer free samples.* If you have treats like chocolate or cookies, people will do anything for a free sample.

5. *Demonstrate a prototype at a public event.*

6. *Stage a free performance exhibition with other artists or musicians.*

7. *Stick balloons and a sign on your car.* Then park it on the street. It's one good legal way to get advertising right out into traffic.

8. *Hang a banner from your dorm room window* (as long as the administration doesn't hang YOU for it).

9. *Dress your dog in a T-shirt with your logo* (or use as many friends' dogs as you can muster).

10. *Put flyers under the windshield wipers of cars.*

11. *Wear an "Ask me about . . ." button.*

12. *Give out lapel pins, stickers, pencils, calendars, etc.*

13. *Tape your flyers to the sidewalk* (most people look down when they walk).

14. *Give "two for the price of one" coupons.*

15. *Get friends and cooperative business owners to display your business card.*

16. *Leave a business card on the bulletin boards in supermarkets.*

17. *Put an ad in the classifieds.* Consider *Entrepreneur* and other magazines.

18. *Join forces with other entrepreneurs on your campus and make a flyer advertising all of your businesses.*

19. *Mention your business on your answering machine.*

20. *Create your own bumper sticker.* Mark Idzik of Strictly Software Plus, Inc., at Georgetown University, has

a personalized license plate that says "SS INC." on his company vehicle—a moped.

21. *Get a magnetic car door sign or have a sign painted on your car.*

22. *Sponsor a triathlete, marathoner, etc., and have him or her wear custom sportswear with your logo.*

23. *Leave tent-shaped mini flyers on cafeteria tables* (with the manager's approval).

24. *Take out an ad with a coupon in programs at football games and other contests.*

25. *Put an ad in the quarterly ACE newspaper.*

And, for the truly ambitious:

26. *Make a promotional videotape.*

27. *Start a newsletter.* Ideal for computer aficionados or specialty hobbyists.

28. *Use computer-based bulletin boards.* Leave short advertisements on data bases that are accessed by home computer owners with telephone modems. I have used them myself to advertise my books and look for student entrepreneurs.

29. *Go in the "back door" for radio and TV airtime.* Community access cable stations are frequently open to young people with an interesting idea. I once got five minutes free of charge on the local station to plug a seminar I was presenting. Also, campus radio stations are targeted to a specific audience—ideal for advertising high-appeal services like food or public events.

30. *Try aerial advertising.* Marc Magor once attached advertising to the underside of his wings when he flew in a hang gliding competition. Consider buying a share in a hot air balloon and put advertising on one of the panels.

Or hire a plane, like the senior class of the Grosse Pointe High School in Detroit, Michigan. They trailed a banner over the graduation ceremony of their arch-rival school that said, "The REAL graduation was yesterday."

7

FROM "THANKS, BUT—" TO "YES, PLEASE!"

How to Open and Close a Sale

"A good name is rather to be chosen
than great riches."
–Proverbs 22:1

PONDERING PROFITS

featuring
Don Carruthers of Food For Thought

When the dorm party's getting crazy and you're almost out of food, there's only one number to call: 587–WILD. On the other end you'll reach Food For Thought, a campus delivery service that students at the University of California, San Diego are eating up.

Food For Thought is run by 23-year-old Don Carruthers. When he transferred from UC Santa Barbara, he was appalled (but delighted) to find that students had no place to go for late-evening munchies. UCSD sits high on a bluff surrounded by 400-foot sea cliffs, million-dollar mansions, and hi-tech corporations. Consequently, tacos and pizzas, standard staples for starving students, just aren't available. An unfulfilled need—such is the stuff entrepreneurial opportunities are made of. Don decided to buy the fledgling Food For Thought Co. from a graduating senior, Dan Klau, who had just started it.

The business concept is simple: Step 1: Stressed-out freshman gets a raving craving for munchies. Step 2: He or she calls Don or leaves an order with his dumb but hardworking partner, the answering machine. Step 3: Don and employees pick up the orders from Roberto's Mexican Food and bring them in large hot boxes to the lobbies of the main dorms. Step 4: Customer crams money in Don's pocket, crams burrito in mouth, and then continues cramming for exams.

The business is so simple: No hassle with preparing food. No Health Department to tangle with. No pots and pans that need washing. The only items required are a business license and tax forms. On a typical night, Food For Thought takes in $50 to $250, averaging about $80 profit for three to five hours' work. But other time is needed for innovative advertising. Don comments that flyers are extremely effective in reaching students, adding, "Newspaper ads are useless."

Like most entrepreneurs, Don has several more schemes ready to go, now that Food For Thought is operating smoothly. He plans to begin an innovative clothing design company that will make workout wear that athletes can literally rip off their bodies when they get too sweaty.

At a science-minded school like UCSD, it's only logical that Don has made a science out of motivation. A student of applied psychology, he uses creative visualization to make his goals more motivating to him in the here-and-now. One technique is called "future pacing," where he makes the object of desire so real in his mind that the image summons up every bit of his resourcefulness to achieve it. He says, "If my goal one week is a car stereo, I keep my mind fixed on the specific goal and imagine how good I will feel once I have it."

Plastered all over his bathroom mirror are notes like "The difference between 'ordinary' and 'extraordinary' is that little extra." To stay motivated, he exercises every day and reads great books like Napoleon Hill's *Think and Grow Rich*. He says, "Every day I fill my mind with empowering thoughts. I give myself a positive mental data dump."

The manager is busier than the Mad Hatter and the White Rabbit combined. She only has a few minutes to see the glossy calendars being presented by the college-age salesman from Design Look, Inc. He merely asks that she listen to a short promotional tape, so she consents. He lets her take control of the machine. Her face shows mild disinterest until she presses the button. Then a voice she could swear is Bogie himself begins:

"Goodbye, Schweetheart. It's been a pleasure . . ."

"No! You can't leave me! And the calendars . . . you can't take the calendars!"

"It's too late, Schweetheart—they're going with me . . ."

The manager's face has changed. The down-turned corners of her mouth have curved into a smile bigger than the Cheshire Cat's. Even before the salesman shows her the samples, she is planning to buy.

The art of selling is an integral part of entrepreneurship.* Sales generate cash flow. Ultimately, nothing happens in business until money changes hands.

Persuasion and selling are one and the same. A service concept or a book idea must be "sold" just as much as a calendar or a Cadillac. Regardless of the nature of the transaction, you must persuade someone to take some course of action. In fact, persuasion plays roles in entrepreneurial success that are seldom considered:

> You must persuade suppliers, moneylenders, parents, and peers that your business is for real;
>
> You must persuade partners or employees to become a motivated, cohesive team;
>
> You must persuade yourself to keep focused on sales goals and habits that produce success.

The ideas in this chapter will be useful in your business, and also in your personal life. The ideas on rapport, sensitivity to body language, and overcoming objections can help you create win/win solutions to family arguments, gain project approval from professors, and maybe even convince a total fox/totally foxy dude to go out with you.

NEW AGE PRINCIPLES FOR SALES SUCCESS

Fill people's needs—elegantly! Take the stereotypical salesman. He sidles up to you in his wingtips and plaid coat and slaps you on the back with an unbearably loud "How ya doin' t'day?" His ulterior motives ooze down his chin as he verbally twists your ear so you'll buy the fan-

---

* In this chapter, "salesperson" is shorthand for saying "entrepreneur acting temporarily in a sales capacity," and "prospect" refers to anyone you need to persuade.

tastic, stupendous, gravity-defying Wonderwidget that slices, dices, and doubles as a paperweight. Low class.

Selling is an honorable activity, but insensitive sales-people give it a bad name. By failing to discover and fill people's true needs, they violate the basic win/win basis of free enterprise: A successful transaction occurs only when both parties are mutually satisfied.

If everyone knew perfectly their wants and how to fill them, the subtle science of selling would be dead. The fact is, many people don't even have the foggiest notion what their needs or wants are in the first place. Therefore, you provide a valuable service to them and society. Help them discover ways to invest in themselves, their families, or their businesses. *That's* elegance.

Get excited! How much thought and energy did you put into creating your product or building your business? How much do you want to enrich your customer's life? How good will you feel after the sale? How can you use the money you're going to earn? Think about these things before you approach a prospect. You may get so wired that the sale will have been made even before you pick up the phone!

Set specific sales strategies. Beth Whiting runs track for her high school in addition to running her hand-painting business. Like all the other runners disciplined enough to make it to the Ohio State track finals, she knows that a total win is made up of a lot of smaller wins. Sales goals are like the time intervals her coach yells out to tell her whether she's running fast enough to make an overall goal. She says, "It takes a lot of hard work, perseverance, and dedication to bring your time down, as well as to succeed in business."

Making sales goals will help keep you (and any people you have selling for you) on track. Set a specific amount and a specific date. For example, write a goal that states, "Gain four new customers by Saturday" or "Sell 75 units by December 24." Like time intervals for runners, specifics will help you stay on track.

Project pride in your product. A salesperson once tried to sell me a used bike. I asked about the brand of derailleur, the alloy the frame was made of, and other important specifications. He just stammered, "Look, all I know is it's a good bike, okay?" I hung up the phone, disgusted.

As the entrepreneur, no one knows your product or service like you. Demonstrate how your service differs from and surpasses the competition in quality or price (known as your "differential advantage"). Find specific ways it meets your customer's particular needs and specifications. Present your product, your service, and especially *yourself* with confidence.

Keep at it. The aerobics workout was one of the most humbling experiences of my life. My male ego took a pounding as women twice my age effortlessly did one leglift after another. I quit at five. When it came to dancing, they leapt and jumped in orchestrated perfection. I flapped my arms like a retarded turkey. Toward the end of an hour and a half of 180-proof pain, I cursed Jane Fonda, excoriated Richard Simmons, and wished Jackie Sorensen upon the devil himself for starting this whole insanity in the first place!

Going to the Total Workout Center was my last-ditch attempt to persuade the aerobics teacher to attend a seminar I was helping to promote. Laura Ann not only decided to go, but later joined the promotion team. As we worked together, she admitted that if I hadn't kept calling her and sending her material to read, she would have let the whole thing drop.

To some people, the word "no" is like water to the Wicked Witch of the West. They shrivel up, clam up, and give up. Leave these would-be persuaders in the unemployment line. Don Carruthers, who has had several sales-intensive businesses, notes, " 'No' just means, 'I don't have enough information yet.' " He goes on to say, "A 'no' is nothing personal. You can generally expect four or five attempts at a close before you get it." He suggests that if one approach doesn't work, try another approach. If that doesn't work, it just means you need to modify your approach some more. If you get a consistent no, it probably means the idea doesn't meet the prospect's needs right now. No problem. Go on to someone else.

THE PSYCHOLOGY OF SELLING

Selling is like fishing, the world's *second* oldest profession. It requires patience, timing, and just a bit of hooking.

Landing a sale takes three steps:

1. Building rapport
2. Discovering needs
3. Closing the sale.

Building rapport   The main difference between a human salesperson and a roadside billboard is a *relationship*. People like to buy from people. It makes them feel special. Despite this fact, many salespeople show about as much sensitivity to their customers as a painted board. They describe and display the product just fine, but they fail to take account of the humanity of the people standing in front of them. Don't be like them. Instead, take the time to get to know your prospects and share some of yourself. Nothing builds rapport as quickly as a smile or a spontaneous and sincere compliment.

In fact, a smile is the best ice-breaker in the world. Most people have a degree of xenophobia, or fear of strangers, and the stranger you are, the more they'll fear you. (Have you ever bought anything from a man with purple hair and a spiked dog collar?) Therefore, when you first meet someone, be as unthreatening as an old friend. Smile and act at ease; he'll mirror your actions. Offer your name and purpose up front, and mention something that puts you on common ground. For example, my friend Doug Sutton, who put together an auto repair discount card offer, introduces himself this way:

"Good evening, I'm Doug Sutton from the Exxon down the street, and we're running a special on auto maintenance some of your neighbors like Mrs. Ciruli have been getting. Would you like to take a look?"

He lets the person hold the card while he explains how, for $20, they can receive $265 worth of free auto maintenance. His easy manner builds rapport from the first moments of conversation, which accounts for why he often makes $50 to $100 in a few hours.

Rapport is based on a subconscious, gut feeling of trust. People enjoy buying from, *and keep on buying from,* people they trust. The only true way to develop long-standing rapport is to give people honest information and follow up any promise, small or large.

But how does someone know he trusts you when he's only just met you?

The answer is astounding, according to recent nontraditional research by Tony Robbins of the Robbins Research Institute, a leading instructor in a field of applied psychology called neurolinguistics. The research confirms what we've known intuitively for a long time: *People who are like each other—like each other.* Who does your prospect know better than anyone else in the world? Himself. And the people he trusts are those most like him. What would happen if you presented yourself in a way he could really relate to?

To build rapport quickly, neurolinguistics offers a simple technique called mirroring. It's simple: Observe the other person's communication style, from the gestures he uses to the tone of his voice, to his pet phrases. Then match them. If he speaks in low tones, speak softly as well. If he leans forward, lean forward as well, *but just slightly.* Just be natural about it. After all, mirroring is something we do already. Have you ever noticed how two friends will sit the same way and use the same vocabulary? Or how one smile begets another? Awareness of the technique will simply help you build rapport with strangers more quickly. If you genuinely respect people and want to help them, this technique will become habit and you will be "unconsciously competent," in Tony Robbins's terminology.

Discovering needs With enough rapport, the other person will tell you all you need to know. All you need to do is listen. What sorts of things does he look for in a product? What kind of service does he expect? Is price important? There is a nonverbal message as well. Is he excitable? Cool and rational? Present your product or service in terms of his style. For example, once I was trying to convince a teenager to buy my book, *High School Superstars.* He didn't want anything to do with school, let alone how to become a high school superstar. I asked him, "What would you look for in a book if you did?" Asking "What if?" opens up a person's imagination.

He laughed. "How to get more girls."

"What if," I opened to a picture of the most beautiful girl in the book, Elizabeth Day, "you could meet a girl like this?"

He took the book into his own hands. He was hooked. I grinned, "Chapters 10 and 11 will tell you everything you ever wanted to know but were afraid to ask." He shoved $10 in my hand and said, "Sign my copy, please."

Closing the sale Buying takes a positive decision. Most people avoid, evade, and procrastinate about making decisions. As a master persuader, do them a favor. Ease them over the hump. They will give you signs that they are ready: fidgeting, clearing their throat, staring at the product. Take note of an ancient Oriental merchant's secret: When the

potential buyer's pupils dilate, they're ready to buy. This is when you should close the sale. Ask, "Can I wrap that one up for you?" Or use the classic "forced choice" close: "Will that be cash or check?"

OVERCOMING OBJECTIONS

The prospect coughs. "Well I . . . I dunno. Maybe not . . ."

Objections are security blankets that people wear to put off that awful act of making a decision. Do them another favor. Replace fears with facts.

If you get, "I'll have to ask my husband," respond with, "Great. What time should I return to talk with him?"

If you get, "I can't afford it right now," offer the prospect an extended payment plan.

If you get, "I would, but I just don't have the time," explain how your product or service will save time.

If the prospect still wavers, sweeten the pot. Doug Sutton offers to throw in a certificate for $10 worth of gasoline (which he would have included anyway). Or, when a parent hesitates at buying one of my books, I offer to write an inscription to the kids. It never fails.

FOLLOWUP

Prospecting for new customers takes time and effort. Up to a point, it's worth it; first-time customers build your business. But it's more important to give TLF (Tender Loving Followup) to the ones you've got. Send them greeting cards at Christmas or make a newsletter for your mailing list. Call up key clients from time to time and ask how they like your product or the job you did. Ask for advice on improving your service, and always ask for referrals.

(Remember the 200-squared rule. If you have 200 customers, each with 200 friends, you have 40,000 potential customers.)

Mastering persuasion takes using these techniques and principles again and again, until they become "unconsciously competent." Use rapport-building, listening for needs, and offering elegant solutions to people's problems in every aspect of your business, not just for sales. Practice them in your personal relationships, too. These habits can help you relate to people better, and can also get you out of a jam.

One time I was on my way to give a speech on the student entrepreneurship movement, and got stuck at the airport for an unexpected layover. I discovered I was very hungry at the same time I discovered I didn't have my wallet on me. All I had were a couple of my books. A little while later, after having good conversations and making some new friends in Arizona, the books were sold and I tamed my growling stomach. It's surprising how resourceful you can be when you're hungry.

A FEW FINAL SALES TIPS

Dress for rapport.   Be like the person you're approaching: business suits for corporate types, jeans for peers.

Take note of names and faces.   A person's name is the most stimulating word in the world to him or her. Use the name often in conversation—you'll remember it easier. Don Carruthers advises getting to know your clients personally. "If you remember little details about their families," he says, "they'll know you think they're important." You may find it worthwhile to keep a customer information file for followup business.

Use visual aids. They can make a sales presentation come alive. If possible, have a case of free samples. All adults have a child within them. Like a 2-year-old in a museum, they like to touch, taste, experience—so let them! For a service business, present a scrapbook of past projects or show a video.

Follow up on commitments immediately (especially those made over the phone).

Reward yourself or your employees after achieving a major sales goal (the motivation level will go through the roof). Don Carruthers writes his sales goals for the week on the wall by his bed. Next to it is his "wish list"—new stereo, new car, etc.—that is contingent on achieving his goals.

Get fired up on motivational reading. I recommend *Think and Grow Rich* by Napoleon Hill, *The Greatest Salesman in the World* by Og Mandino, and the audio libraries of Nightingale-Conant Corp. (see Appendix A).

8

LAUGHING ALL THE WAY TO THE BANK
Bookkeeping and Cash Management

"Money is like an arm or a leg—use it or lose it."
—Henry Ford

PLAYING ANTI-MONOPOLY

featuring
Ken Appel of KB Books

"David vs. Goliath" the headline read. The cover story of the *UCSD Guardian* featured not a Biblical showdown, but a very contemporary battle between a group of student entrepreneurs and a highly profitable arm of the University of California, San Diego. "David" was KB Books, a small and strong student bookselling enterprise threatening "Goliath," the monopoly of the multimillion-dollar University Bookstore.

KB Books was established in the summer of 1984 when Ken Appel, Don Sheffler, and Paul Martinelli decided they were sick and tired of paying exorbitant prices for required textbooks. With the University Bookstore charging 6 percent or more over list price—more than any other University of California bookstore—they calculated they could offer books to students for 10 percent under the competition and still make a profit.

At first the hassles for KB Books loomed at least as large as the infamous Goliath. Obtaining credit, for example: Even after securing a valid San Diego business license, the owners found it hard to get a bank to take them seriously. However, when Ken Appel's father promised to provide the collateral for all the loans, KB Books was allowed to borrow enough capital to make its initial book purchases.

Getting prospective customers to take them seriously was their next test. Their first sales came from books sold out of the back of their car. Matt DeTeresa, who joined Ken and the others early on in the business, remembers, "People would ask, 'What are you going to do, take my money and run?' Some would even ask, 'What's the catch? Are these stolen books?' "

To solve these problems, Ken tried to get a booth on UCSD's Revelle Plaza, a popular gathering place for students and student entrepreneurs alike. A sales booth is legal there if it is sponsored by a student organization. Ken worked out a deal with student government that gave them 8 percent of the net, or pretax, profits. In exchange, KB Books would have a booth and the legal right to operate a business. Simple, right?

Wrong. Enter Goliath. The University Bookstore insisted that it had the exclusive right to sell books on the campus, and threatened to call in the police.

It was all a bluff. UCSD is a large university, and has its own student legal services. Ken checked with them and found out the "exclusive right" claim was without substance. He filed a petition with university officials, asking them to honor the agreement with student government.

As expected, the proposal got lost in the bureaucratic shuffle. KB Books took it as an opportunity to move off campus. They opened a small store close to UCSD, which grossed $28,000 in its first 15 weeks.

After winning that battle, they decided to expand to San Diego State University; this involved purchasing a $20,000 computerized bookkeeping system and taking on a marketing partner, Blair LeMire. Their current goal is to capture 20 percent of the student textbook market, worth about $750,000 a year. With outrageous promos like live remote broadcasting at their book sales from XTRA-FM (a local radio station), notebook giveaways, and a run of 40,000 flyers, they are making a mark on San Diego State's book buying habits. Blair explains, "We're trying to put pizzazz in the book business."

To the creative entrepreneurial mind, bookkeeping seems like a bureaucratic chore that keeps an entrepreneur from going out and making real money. For me, bookkeeping was so intimidating I'd do anything— wash the dishes, take out the garbage, even STUDY—before I'd open my ledger and record the day's or week's accounts. After comparing notes with other entrepreneurs, I finally admitted I really didn't want to face reality. Like many others, I didn't want to know if I was losing money.

What I discovered, when I finally set my mind to doing it right, was that bookkeeping isn't nearly as hard as it may seem. It doesn't take much time if you stay on top of it regularly.

For any business, keeping good business records serves three valuable purposes that translate into real money in the long run.

Immediate cash management   Keeping a close eye on how much cash you have, your accounts payable (how much you owe), and your accounts receivable (how much others owe you) means you have more control and peace of mind. You know whether you can afford new equipment or goods, and you don't bounce checks. Verne Harnish of ACE warns that failing to keep records regularly "is like playing basketball and not giving the score till the end of the game."

Long-range business decisions   If you know how much money is being spent on which items, and know which services or products are bringing you the most income, you can adjust your management strategies to reduce costs and increase profit.

Tax preparation   Consistent, well-organized bookkeeping will make calculating your taxes a cinch, and you'll have the peace of mind that comes when you know you're paying the fair and honest amount.

If, despite these benefits, bookkeeping still seems like an awful chore, remember: your books don't care who keeps them. They will be perfectly content if you let a partner, employee, or accounting service take care of them. An entrepreneur is simply *not* an accountant. Just make sure you're out there hustling to create cash flow in the first place.

Ken Appel, whose business is book-keeping in the literal sense, advises, "Sure, bookkeeping's a drag and no one wants to do it, but it's important. Get someone who knows what he or she is doing."

BOOKKEEPING SYSTEMS

Bookkeeping systems range from spiral-bound notebooks to sophisticated computerized accounting systems. In my high school lawn service, I got by at first with a pad I kept in my pocket! A good bet for a beginning student enterprise is simply recording *all* expenses in your business checking account. Your check stubs provide a reliable, easily traceable record of expenses. A slightly more sophisticated approach is the single-entry ledger. A popular ledger I recommend is the *Dome Simplified Weekly Bookkeeping Record*, which can be found in any office supply store. Once a week, you classify your expenses into categories such as inventory, travel, advertising, etc. This is necessary for tax purposes and helps you monitor your spending trends. Cash already received and cash still owed is recorded separately. Keep these accounts in a separate ledger or invoice book. (See "Billing," below.)

As soon as it becomes practical for you, begin using a computer for keeping records. A good program will be able to handle accounts receivable, accounts payable, cut a check, itemize expenses, and keep a running total. Business accounting software is readily available in stores. It may be less expensive just to design your own computer program or have a friend write one that is made just for you.

RECEIPTS AND OTHER PAPER RECORDS

Any business needs a filing system. Important documents can be kept in a small filing box, and the rest can be filed along with junk mail in the most efficient file of all, the "round file." If most of your records are kept on disk, you won't need a very big filing system. A portable briefcase-sized one is quite versatile and can be purchased for a couple of dollars from your local office supply store. Some typical file headings include:

Accounts receivable (invoices)
Accounts payable (bills to pay)
Product brochures
Warranties (on your main business equipment)
Tax forms
Licenses
Insurance
Bank statements
Cancelled checks
Clippings (or keep a scrapbook of publicity on your business)
Paid bills and receipts (use a separate folder for each month).

Note: It is important for tax purposes that you keep a paper receipt of each purchase. Your cancelled checks and expense ledger are not quite good enough for the IRS if you get audited, so make it a habit to save *every* receipt.

BILLING

In a cash-and-carry business like selling Frisbees at the beach, paperwork can be as minimal as your customers' swimwear. In a moderately sophisticated business, however, sometimes it's the best use of time to deliver first and collect payment later. For example, I collected my fee every two or four weeks from my lawn customers. A simple system to use is a carbon-copy receipt, or the computer equivalent. At the time your customers receive the goods or the service, agree on a time by which payment must be received. (Thirty days is standard.) Give one slip to the customer and keep one for yourself. Most people pay on time, some pay when they get around to it, and a few need at least two phone calls. For this reason, choose your credit risks very carefully.

For paying your own bills, set aside one day per month to do it. I pay all my bills at once at the end of the month so that my bookkeeping, checkbook balancing, and invoice sending happens all at once.

BANKING

Choose a good bank, because you'll be laughing all the way there if your enterprise is successful. A good bank should have a convenient location, electronic banking, a

helpful staff, and good interest rates. If you can find one where interest is paid on your checking account, or where there is no service charge (which is often over 20 cents per check), so much the better.

You should set up two business accounts in addition to your personal accounts. *Do not* mix your personal and business accounts or your finances will become muddier than the Mississippi in May. Your business checking account will consist of a book of oversize checks with stubs for instant recordkeeping. It typically costs more than a regular checking account and may require a state seller's permit, business license, and DBA (statement explained in the next chapter). Therefore, consider opening a personal checking account and using it for business purposes. Also, open a savings account at the same time and make it a habit to save money on a regular basis.

AM I REALLY MAKING MONEY?

The bottom line of business is profit (or loss). To determine your net profit at the end of a quarter or at the end of the year, simply make this calculation:

Gross Profit Equals Gross Receipts (Money Taken In)
Minus Gross Expenses (Money Spent)

For example, if Jerry sold ten doghouses in 1987 at $50 each, his income would be $500. Suppose paint, wood, and other business expenses amounted to $200. Profit is $300.

Gross expenses consist of the cost of your goods and the cost of doing business. Be sure to count only the goods you bought during the current calendar year as "the cost of goods." Other details, such as depreciation (spreading out the cost of large investments across several years) and deductions for college tuition, will be discussed in the next chapter.

Using the books for business planning. Adding up the totals of cash received and accounts receivable against the itemized expenses should reveal some trends. Are you making a profit? Is the product or service marked up high enough (or low enough) to yield maximum profit? Is a lot of money spent on business expenses that aren't paying for themselves in the long run? A simple method taught in basic business textbooks is the "break-even chart."

BREAK-EVEN POINT

The break-even point represents the point where income (sales) equals expenses (variable and fixed). Before your company reaches this point, you will be operating at a loss. After you have passed this point, you'll be making a profit. One method to calculate your company's break-even point is shown on page 121.

Many computer programs will allow you to play with different hypothetical pricing strategies and other business decisions. The reality is that business forecasting at our level is more of an art than a science. The best plan is to get a lot of advice from different sources and follow your gut feeling.

GETTING ADVICE

Even learning the simplest of bookkeeping procedures is sometimes frustrating. Check out what systems other student entrepreneurs are using. Other sources for advice on bookkeeping and management in general include:

SCORE The Service Corps of Retired Executives is a free and confidential business consulting service run by the Small Business Administration (SBA). Make an appointment to talk with one of the counselors. If your counselor is anything like the San Diego SCORE professionals, he or she will be friendly and knowledgeable.

A local businessperson Offer to spend some time helping someone in exchange for teaching you field-tested ideas and insight. Campus entrepreneur clubs often have "mentor programs" for this purpose. Otherwise, your local chamber of commerce may be able to set you up with such a person.

Professors Many of your instructors may have had experience in the business world before teaching. If they can ever get past the theory, they will probably give you sound advice!

Parents If both parents were entrepreneurs, like mine were, you may get more good advice than you can absorb at a time. But even if they haven't been in business, they might have good general advice on things like insurance and taxes.

Publications The Internal Revenue Service (IRS) and the SBA are excellent resources for short practical pamphlets. Also, libraries and bookstores have thousands of how-to business books (see Appendix A).

Lawyers, accountants, and consultants Only consult them if you absolutely need professional advice and can afford $15 to $100 an hour, or if you have a family contact.

SELLING YOUR BUSINESS

Entrepreneurs have a restless spirit that makes them keep moving on to bigger and better things. Selling your business

---

BREAK-EVEN POINT

Sales Price ～～～～～
Minus Cost Per Unit − ～～～～～
Equals Markup Per Unit = ～～～～～

$$\frac{\text{Fixed Costs} ～～～～～}{\text{Markup Per Unit} ～～～～～} = \text{Break-even Point} ～～～～～$$

This also can be shown graphically. To construct the graph,
1. Enter the fixed costs for the year as a base cost line ($500 in the example).
2. Plot the variable expenses line (material and commissions).
3. Plot the sales income line. The break-even point is the intersection of the income and expense lines. At this point (140 units for the sample company), income is equal to expense.

Potential profit (darker area on graph) may be increased by raising prices, increasing sales, or lowering expenses.

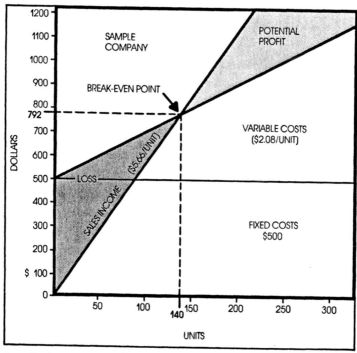

Source: *The Junior Achievement Company Manual*

is the final reward for all the unpaid hours you put into it. Experts suggest that it is much better to sell a business when sales are showing an upward trend. Buyers will pay much more for something that has a positive future. And it's a good feeling to have started something and see it continue after you're gone.

The key is to find someone *worthy* to carry it on. A partner or an employee is the logical choice, but make sure whoever buys the business understands it is a business deal, not a gift.

In selling to—or buying out—a partner, the following buy-sell agreement is standard among entrepreneurs: *If one partner wants to buy out the other, he or she must submit the offer in writing. The other partner, on receiving the offer, automatically has the right to buy out the partner who submitted the offer, at the same price.*

The genius of this agreement (which should be signed when two entrepreneurs first decide to become partners) is that the offerer will be forced to submit a fair price. If not, he or she will be the one bought out!

Valuing the business is, again, an art. If you have a small-scale enterprise, simply sell it for what a buyer is willing to pay. A general rule of thumb is to add up all the assets you will turn over: equipment, office supplies, etc., put a price on "customer good will," and total it up. Use all your skills of persuasion (Chapter 7) to instill your original vision in the buyer. Urge him or her to make it grow, and then sell out for more than what he or she is currently paying. Include, as part of the selling price, all the training and advice the buyer wants.

Then go for it all over again.

9

SAM'S YOUR UNCLE, NOT YOUR BIG BROTHER

A Demystification of Legal and Tax Concerns

"Idleness and pride tax with a heavier hand than kings and parliaments. If we can get rid of the former, we may easily bear the latter."
—Benjamin Franklin

TAKING IT TO THE STREET

featuring
Dave and Stephen Goldman of MacProducts,
Inc.

Back when all the teenyboppers were ogling Farrah
Fawcett, shelling out for KISS concerts, and feeding
their parents' quarters into pinball machines, David
Goldman was busy buying and selling coins and
his brother Stephen was digging up rocks and selling them to neighbors. Later, when David was at
the University of Texas at Austin, they decided to
put their entrepreneurial talents together. Their col-
laboration created MacProducts, a healthy enterprise that will top $4 million dollars before they
graduate.

MacProducts is a thriving computer accessories
business that David and Stephen operate just across
the street from the main campus. Their cash flow,
sometimes $45,000 a day, makes the cost of college
look like the price of a theater ticket. Handling
$250,000 a month has become routine for David
and Stephen, who are 23 and 22, respectively.

Like many other student-created businesses,
MacProducts began by accident. One day in Feb-

125

ruary 1985, David and Stephen decided to order some computer disks for their Apple Macintosh. Discovering a few extras, they passed some on to their friends. In no time they were deluged with requests for more disks, and they began ordering in larger quantities. They moved the operations out of their apartment and into a store and hired three students as employees. They teamed up with an accountant because they knew that his financial expertise would be a team asset.

Business is growing at a pace only true entrepreneurs could handle; it already has passed the $3 million mark. However, the owners have yet to draw much money out of their store, as they reinvest nearly every dollar. David remarks, "That's ironic, since it started out as something to make a little money on the side."

An engineering/business major, David finds that running a business has really improved his understanding of the market. He remarks, "Sometimes you'll be sitting in class and hear a prof say, 'Such-and-so is impossible.' Except you know it *is* possible because you've actually done it yourself!" MacProducts is often brought up in class by professors as a case study, and almost daily, complete strangers accost them in the hall to ask how business is going.

They believe running a business as students gives them a very valuable experience in dealing with the real world. It's taught them the "real thing" in budgeting, decision making, and bouncing back from problems. One $3,000 investment in floppy disks was a complete flop. David figures it's all part of his learning experience. He laughed, "At least it wasn't $30,000!"

An entrepreneur's nightmare was once put on film in the award-winning movie, *The Incredible Bread Machine*. Once upon a time a man named Tom Smith invented a machine that produced thousands of loaves of bread an hour. Loaf upon loaf rolled off the conveyor belt—enough to feed the whole world.

Then the government stepped in. It regulated and taxed, delayed and deterred, restricted and constricted the incredible bread machine until it squeaked to a halt. Tom was thrown in jail.

The threat of paperwork, legal hassles, and taxation prevents many would-be student entrepreneurs from leaving the paperwork, legal hassles, and taxation of paid employment. Don't let such false fears stop you. The threat seems bigger than it is for two reasons.

First, student-run enterprises are often so small or informal that they can get by with almost no legal problems. For example, in a small on-campus typing service, you may only have to get permission from a campus authority to post your flyers.

Second, even if you do plan to run a legitimate business that deals with the "outside world," legalities will not take too much time or worry if you get good advice from other entrepreneurs and how-to books.

A word of warning: A cavalier attitude toward laws and the "powers that be" could get you and your business slammed like a mosquito. Take the time to learn which legalities apply to you and take care of them with a minimum of fuss so that you can get on to more important things. The purpose of this chapter is not to explain every detail of the law, but to acquaint you with some basic legal aspects of business that apply to student entrepreneurs.

LEGAL PAPERWORK: THE BASICS

Business licenses   A business license is required so that your enterprise is recognized as a legal business, and it is issued by your local city or county government. The cost varies from place to place. For example, in Santa Clara, California, the cost was $50 per year for Brett Kingstone's bedding warehouse. To get a business license, visit your city hall (listed in the government listings in the first section of your phone book) and fill out the form. Do it before you start your business operations, since there can be a delinquent fee.

On an ill-fated trip Doug Melinger and David Goldsmith took to Fort Lauderdale, they ran into some unexpected legal problems. David explains, "The first day we started selling, the police came over. They told us we would need a business license, which they said would be about $300. It ended up being about $35. Then they came back and told us it was the wrong one. Then we had to go back and get a few hundred thousand dollars' worth of sidewalk and liability insurance. We were going to do it legal from the start. I think we were the first two people in history to go down to Fort Lauderdale and do that."

Fictitious business name statement or "doing business as" (DBA)   Unless your business name is your own (e.g., Van Hutchinson, speaker/author), you will have to file a DBA with the county government. Its twofold purpose is to 1) give customers a way to track down unscrupulous people hiding behind a fictitious business name, and 2) prove your business name is unique within a certain region. You must file your DBA statement in the local newspaper once a week for four weeks. The filing cost at the county clerk is affordable ($10 in California). The newspaper will charge between $15 and $40, and sometimes it pays for itself as if it were advertising. Proof of a DBA is usually required to establish a business checking account.

State seller's permit   If you plan to sell a retail product directly to consumers in a state where state sales tax is collected, you will need this permit. On the other hand, if you only perform services, or sell only to wholesalers, or sell food, or sell only out-of-state, you will not need it. This permit gives you the right to collect sales tax, which you must pay to the state four times a year. The advantage of this permit is that you can buy merchandise from your wholesaler without having to pay tax on it yourself. In California, the permit can be obtained at no charge from the local office of the State Board of Equalization, but you have to go in person. Furthermore, many types of businesses require substantial deposits—$250 or more—so ask beforehand.

Employer's registration form   If you plan to hire employees, you need to register as an employer with the state and federal governments. In California, you simply include this information on your application for a seller's permit. For the federal government, you will be assigned a Federal Employer Number once you register. File Form SS–4 with the Internal Revenue Service to get this number. Once your form is filed, the IRS will automatically send you quarterly and yearly payroll tax forms. You will also need to obtain proof of your Social Security number and those of your employees, available by filing Form SS–5. You should also request the necessary forms for W–2 and W–4 statements for your employees. There are also many other legal requirements to wade through if you choose to have employees rather than independent contractors. Get sound advice.

Zoning and other regulations   Most student entrepreneurs run their businesses out of their homes or dorm rooms and don't need to worry about zoning, fire and safety inspections, etc. If you plan to run a food business, you will need an inspection from the Health Department. All these procedures take time—it took two months before Brett Kingstone could get his business license for his bedding warehouse because of the routine inspections that were required.

Running a business on campus has always been a bone of contention between student entrepreneurs and institutions, who tend to look down their noses at the idea of students bringing free enterprise within the gates of the ivory tower. Most student entrepreneurs just keep quiet and no one cares as long as they do not violate basic decency or use school resources for personal profit. (There is a difference between making sales calls on your dorm telephone and opening an exotic pet shop on the premises.)

However, if the issue is forced, as in the case of KB Books, you have four alternatives: to go underground, move the operation off-campus, pay the university a share of the profits, or simply thumb your nose at it and continue as before—but get legal advice first!

Insurance　In certain fields you may need liability insurance or bonding. This is your assurance to customers that if they or their property is damaged, your insurance will pay. Needless to say, this is very expensive and probably will not be necessary until your business is very large. One way around it is the use of waivers: Marc Magor has his hang gliding students sign a form that releases him from liability if they get hurt. You should definitely get legal advice before using a form like this.

Patents and copyrights　The moment you create a literary work, write new software, or invent a product, the law says it is your "intellectual property." However, to secure a copyright that will hold up in a court of law, you must file with the Copyright Office, Library of Congress, Washington, D.C. 20559. Write to the Library for information, then send the $10 processing fee along with two copies of your work. If you sign a contract with a publishing company, be sure your contract secures the copyright in *your* name.

Patenting can get expensive. Count on several hundred dollars for filing and lawyers' fees. The whole process could take as much as two years. But if your invention is good, it's worth it. Later you may be able to sell out for thousands, perhaps millions, of dollars.

Incorporation　This is very complicated and can cost more than $600 in legal fees. It can be worthwhile IF you have had experience in business, if you need to raise capital by selling stock, or you want to protect personal assets in the case of bankruptcy. Read widely and get sound advice.

FACTS ABOUT TAXES

I don't know anyone who jumps for joy and sings "Yankee Doodle" at the thought of paying taxes, but in a sense it's a good sign: the enterprise is healthy enough to move into the black and turn a profit.

Much of the fear about taxes is unfounded. In truth, paying taxes is

fairly simple,

a "real-world" education, and

a way to claim deductions as a business owner that the average wage earner can't (such as certain educational expenses).

In general, small businesses do not pay taxes on profits. Their owners do. Uncle Sam taxes only individuals and corporations, not proprietorships and partnerships. However, the business entity is responsible for other taxes, such as sales tax, employment tax, etc.

If your business enterprise is small, you may not need to pay any tax at all. As of 1987, your business income must exceed $400 to be taxable for FICA, or Social Security (see "Federal self-employment tax," below). To be required to pay federal personal income tax on Form 1040 (the one you've probably heard your folks complain about), your income from your business profits and other sources (investments, part-time jobs, etc.) must exceed $4440. Again, since tax reform has thrown a monkey wrench into the system, check with knowledgeable sources about your tax situation. The pertinent IRS publications are especially helpful.

Consistent, accurate bookkeeping will plainly show whether the business made a profit (which may be taxed) or loss (which is not taxed). In special cases a loss may be carried over to offset gains in future years, thus reducing future taxes.

The explanation of how to fill out the forms is on the tax forms themselves. You will probably need Form 1040 (Personal Income Tax) and Schedule C (Profit or Loss from Business or Profession). A bookkeeping ledger, such as the *Dome* system mentioned in the last chapter, will help you determine the profit on which you will be taxed.

The forms for paying taxes often are available at local post offices and some public libraries. If they do not have the forms you need, get them from your local IRS office, listed in the government pages in the front part of your phone book.

DEDUCTIONS FOR STUDENT ENTREPRENEURS

One of the nice little perks of being self-employed is the privilege of deducting legitimate business expenses from your gross receipts. The tax code is very specific on these items, and good tax preparation guides such as the annual *The Arthur Young Tax Guide* can pay for themselves immediately. Check with the guides and qualified persons carefully, as many of these deductions may be eliminated, limited or phased out with the 1987 changes in the tax code.

On the form, the deductions should correspond to the business expense categories you have been using in your ledger. You will need to transfer them from your books to Schedule C of the federal income tax. Here are some distinctions that are relevant to student entrepreneurs:

Education U.S. Treasury Regulation 1, 162–5 states that all educational expenses that improve your professional skills are tax deductible. This means you legally can deduct educational expenses such as books, courses, university fees, commuting expenses, etc., if they improve your professional skills (but not if they prepare you for a new profession). While an art class may not be deductible (unless you are a self-employed artist), courses such as economics, management, business computing, etc., are definitely allowable.

The 1987 laws are *very* strict. Read IRS booklets carefully.

Depreciation This allows businesses to spread out the cost of important equipment across several years. Without it, you would have to lump most of your expenses into the first year when your profits (and taxes) are still comparatively low. Depreciation helps lower your tax in the more profitable years that follow.

For example, if you paid $1,000 for a computer system in 1988 and counted the whole expense in your 1988 taxes, you may not deduct any money for it in 1989. But if you depreciate it over five years, divide the purchase price by five. (Deduct $200 per year until and including 1992.) Note the ACRS and MACRS rates (depreciation tables in IRS tax books) active beginning in 1987.

Note that if you declare the full purchase price for an item as a business expense, you may not depreciate it over several years. More information can be found in IRS publication 534, "Tax Information on Depreciation."

Car expenses Yes, that new Chevy you've been eyeing qualifies as a business expense—if you use it strictly for business. If you use it for business *and* personal use, you have to keep a mileage log and you may deduct only business mileage. (In 1987 the maximum allowable deduction ranged from 11 cents to 22.5 cents a mile, depending on mileage.)

Entertainment A warning to cavalier student entrepreneurs who want to wine and dine as a business expense: "Entertainment" applies only to entertaining your customers or business associates while discussing business matters. (Of course that interesting redhead might *become* a business associate . . .) And, to make matters worse, only 80 percent of legitimate business entertainment expenses are deductible beginning in 1987.

FILLING OUT THE FORMS

State sales tax This tax is applicable only to retail businesses, not service and wholesale businesses. Even better, it doesn't really come out of your pocket, but from your customers'. It is typically paid quarterly (April 30, July 30,

October 30, and January 30). The form is quite simple, but it does require you keep track of how many goods are sold within the state and to collect sales tax on each unit sold. (I was very pleased to discover that items sold to a person in a different state, such as mail-order books, are not subject to sales tax, though a "use tax" may be imposed in the purchaser's state of residence.)

Federal self-employment tax   A common fallacy is that if you're self-employed, you don't have to pay Social Security tax. Wrong. You must pay this tax if you expect profits from the business to be $400 or more. The income generated from self-employment is taxed at a rate of 12.3 percent for 1987, and 13.02 in 1988. You are also taxed separately on your income. This tax is recorded as "paid" at the end of the year using Form 1040, Schedule SE, but the actual money is paid out throughout the year using Form 1040–ES, explained below. IRS Publication 505 has more information.

Estimated tax   This is government's way of hitting you up for a tax four times a year, and it works the same way a withholding program would if you were employed by someone else. If you expect to owe more than $500 tax (1987 figure), you must file Form 1040–ES. This tax is paid quarterly on or before April 15, June 15, September 15, and January 15. The amount of the payment is based on what you predict your income for the coming year will be. Note that these payments cover both your self-employment tax (FICA, or Social Security) and income tax, so be sure to take credit for these payments when you prepare the end-of-the-year 1040 and 1040 SE. Depending on how well you have estimated, you will either get back a refund or will have to pay additional money. When you get form 1040–ES, there will be four vouchers to tear off and send with payment on the appropriate date, so be sure to keep this in your tax folder and mark these dates on your calendar.

State income taxes and self-employment taxes   You might get lucky; some states don't even have income tax. Check with your local chamber of commerce. If they do exist in your state, the forms are almost exactly like the federal forms, and are available through the state income tax office or local post offices. Instructions come with the forms.

Partnerships   Taxpaying for partnerships is quite simple. The partners simply fill out Federal Form 1065, which is almost exactly like Form 1040, Schedule C. No tax is paid by the partnership itself. Instead, the partners split the profit according to an agreed-upon ratio (50/50, 60/40, etc.) and report the income on their own personal income tax, Form 1040. They also jointly file Form 1065, and in some circumstances Schedule K. See IRS Publication 541, "Tax Information on Partnership Income and Losses."

Corporate taxes   These taxes are considerably more complex and beyond the scope of this book. Consult an accountant and use IRS Publication 542, "Corporations and the Federal Income Tax," as a start.

Payroll taxes   The tax requirements for hiring employees are staggering. If you pursue this route, you will become familiar with W–2, W–3, and W–4 Forms for withholding employee taxes, as well as Form 941 and 940. These are explained in IRS Publication 15, "Employer's Tax Guide." Payroll taxes must be paid quarterly to the state and federal governments, and provisions must be made for unemployment and disability insurance.

Note: If you have employees, set aside their Social Security and employee taxes in a separate bank account, and don't touch it! (That money belongs to the government, the most powerful and inflexible creditor you could have.)

A much simpler route is to hire independent contractors. This means the people who work for you are considered self-employed and you don't have to tangle with W–2s and the like. You can't escape the paper shuffle completely, however. You still need to file Federal Form 1099, "Statement of Miscellaneous Earnings," and Form 1096, "Annual Summary and Transmittal of U.S. Information Returns" for each independent contractor.

HELP!

Doing taxes can be a harrowing adventure the first time, and there's no need to gnaw off all your fingernails trying to figure out the system alone. You can get help from the local Small Business Administration and its free counseling service, SCORE. Or you might ask a friend of the family who is in business to explain more about taxes, or you might find it worth the money to hire an accountant.

Your local IRS office has many useful publications. Call them and ask them to send you what you need or stop by in person. Look in your phone book, in the government section, for your local toll-free IRS number. (In San Diego, the number is quite appropriately 1-800-424-1040!) Publications of use to student entrepreneurs include:

Publication 17 Your Federal Income Tax
Publication 334 Tax Guide for Small Business
Publication 505 Tax Withholding and Declaration
of Estimated Tax

Publication	508	Education Expenses
Publication	535	Tax Information on Business Equipment and Operating Losses
Publication	539	Withholding Taxes and Reporting Requirements
Publication	541	Tax Information on Partnership Income and Losses
Publication	587	Business Use of Your Home
Publication	1066	Small Business Tax Workbook.

A word on honesty: It's fashionable to try to cheat the government with a line like "It would only go to a bunch of bureaucrats." That is partly true. But taxes also build roads, feed Grandpa, and put half of your peers through school.

If you are running a *very* small enterprise, it may be both smart and ethical to save yourself and the government the hassle of a lot of unnecessary paperwork by skipping such things as the estimated tax and reporting your small profit on your regular personal income tax.

Taxes are a hassle, but they need not be emotionally taxing. Just look at the whole thing as an adventure, like an all-expenses-deducted trip to bureaucrat-land. We've all got to do it sometime. Why not learn now, when we've got the energy?

10

MANAGING THE WIN/WIN WAY

New Styles of Entrepreneurial Leadership

"None of us is as smart as all of us."
—Pierre Teilhard de Chardin,
The Phenomenon of Man

SUMMING UP THE PARTS

featuring
Karl Edelmann of Edelkinder GMBH

A million and eight auto parts. That's how many parts a group of kids aged 9 to 16 manufactured in their first year in business. They are all equal partners in Edelkinder GMBH. Karl Edelmann, the president, explains, "Edelkinder GMBH is German for The Edelmann Children's Corporation."

They owe much of their success to their father, an immigrant with years of experience in the automotive manufacturing field. He helped them get set up in 1978 making auto parts for General Motors. Edelkinder GMBH made a healthy profit its first year of $20,000 that was split equally among each of the partners: Karl, Ken, Kurt, Kevin, and Kathy. A few years later they had to completely change the business. "Our main product was drying up," Karl says. "We saw the handwriting on the wall. We knew we had to do something or close up shop. So we put our money into a transmission filter for a completely different segment of the auto industry."

Now 26, Karl still heads the company. When

business is going smoothly, his role as president requires only about six hours a week. In fact, he is more likely to be seen in a physician's smock than a business suit. He is a third-year resident at the University of Michigan Medical School.

The early days weren't so "Club Med." Karl was sometimes frustrated by family dissensions that carried over into business. He says, "Family relations are sometimes very helpful to get started in business or get you out of a jam. But later they tend to hold back the company."

Another headache came from unscrupulous suppliers and buyers. "Some were out to make a quick buck off a 'stupid kid'," he complains. "I learned you have to go with your gut feelings. You have to stay aware of what's going on and deal only with people you like and want to deal with."

Playing hardball with the big boys, Karl learned some business lessons quicker than a fastball reaches the mitt. He has a favorite horror story: "In 1981, my customer in Toledo needed parts on a 'yesterday' basis. I rented a large truck, drove to Detroit, and picked up a bin of parts. When I arrived, I found I had picked up the wrong parts. I turned around, only to have the truck die six blocks from my final destination.

"I got up the next morning and rented a new truck. By now my customer needed his parts on a 'day-before-yesterday' basis. I found this truck, too, was slowing down. I finally got a U-Haul and got the parts to Toledo. In the end, everyone was satisfied; not necessarily happy, but satisfied."

Being the head of a company has its advantages and disadvantages, says Karl. "With a 9-to-5 job you may have a boss and maybe even a few people under you. But in a business, you are your own boss, which can be scary as hell at times. You can't say, 'That's not my job. Talk to so-and-so.'"

Your business is expanding like the Big Bang all over again. There are new leads to follow up, old customers' problems to handle, miscellaneous trash that says "IRS" to file. All by yourself. And that damn phone keeps ringing till you want to smash it.

What do you do?

Alternatives include:

1. Heap on more work, study less, and get four hours of sleep a night;
2. Cut back activities or shut down business;
3. Run off screaming into the night.

Or you could try cloning yourself. But since that is currently unfeasible, consider the next best thing: Use OPT—other peoples' talent. Marc Magor says it best. "One person is not a master of everything. Success comes through people."

The theme of this chapter is that success in business ultimately rests on resourceful use of an asset more important than money, ideas, and even time: human resources.

The radical fact of human resourcefulness is that one person might be well-capitalized and have a stinging hot idea and still fail if he or she cannot interact well with people; yet another who starts out on a shoestring with a more modest idea, but knows how to network and promote teamwork, might succeed miraculously.

So never let your perceived limitations stop you: *If you don't have it or can't do it, no problem. Just find someone who can.* Read that last sentence again—it just might contain the most important idea of this whole chapter. As Tony Robbins, a motivational speaker, says: "Wealth and power are not so much what you 'have' but what you can get *access* to."

Since student entrepreneurship almost always starts out as a phenomenon that is low-keyed, spontaneous, and definitely not "by the book," carefully evaluate how the following alternatives meet your particular needs.

SOLE PROPRIETORSHIP

Almost all student entrepreneurs traditionally have started out by themselves, expanding as they went along. (There are a few exceptions, of course. My very first business venture was a partnership: My sister and I set up a lemonade stand when I was 6 and she was 9.)

The obvious advantage of sole proprietorship is that it keeps control in your hands. You have responsibility for your own actions only, and there are no complications with payroll, communications, tax and legal hassles, and other headaches too large for a tiny enterprise.

However, consider that going it alone can have the drawbacks we know all too well: Limited capital, limited ideas, limited time (and ability to go on vacation), and ultimately, limited growth. (Note: These perceived limitations are not inevitable. Networking can give you the best of both worlds; more below.)

PARTNERSHIP

Partnership is an alternative that is becoming more common as the student entrepreneurship movement continues to gain sophistication. This is primarily because student entrepreneurs who listen and read widely are discovering what experienced businesspeople have been saying for years: A good partnership is almost always more successful than even the best single entrepreneur. The shared resources such as capital, time, ideas, and moral support can potentially create *synergy*—where the whole is greater than the sum of the individual parts. David and Stephen Goldman, who are brothers as well as partners, attribute their success to dividing their responsibilities effectively.

To get the synergistic effect, each partner's strengths have to make up for the other's weaknesses. If Mrs. Yin is great at making contacts and dreaming up promotion schemes, and Mr. Yang is great at bookkeeping and organizing, they will be a perfect complement. The students in this book have proved this over and over again: While David Goldman is the computer buff of MacProducts, his brother Stephen handles many of the daily business details, such as phone calls, customer service, and new business leads. They divide their responsibilities and also stay out of each other's hair.

On the down side, a partnership potentially can create uncertainty over control. Unawareness of basic human relations can result in flake-outs, shake-outs, walk-outs, and other problems like arguments, unequal commitment, inefficiency of communication, letdowns, and every other ailment of poor communication. (See Chapter 11.)

Partnerships and marriage have so much in common, it's scary. Dan Bienenfeld, who has been in many business "marriages," comments: "If you're spending 8, 10, 12 hours a day with someone, you see your partner more than a spouse."

For choosing partners, Dan Bienenfeld advises student entrepreneurs to find someone who is in business or has been already. He suggests, "Sit down with the prospective person and write down your goals independently. Project what you want to happen in the next five years. Then compare what you've written. Are your goals congruent? Are your styles compatible?"

The choice of a partner is without a doubt the deciding factor in whether the partnership will succeed. Dan philosophizes, "Money's not the name of the game. It's got to be fun." (See "Choosing a Compatible Business Partner," below.)

THE ENTREPRENEURIAL TEAM

An entrepreneurial team simply is a partnership of more than two partners. Family businesses such as Edelkinder GMBH are the oldest kind of entrepreneurial team, but the late 80s are seeing an increase in the number of cooperative enterprises. The ACE club I started at UCSD basically was a cooperative entrepreneurial team. Cooperative enterprises, where companies owned in part or entirely by worker/entrepreneurs are competing within the free enterprise system, are the wave of the future. (See Chapter 14.)

An entrepreneurial team operates like a souped-up partnership. It is the same as a simple partnership, except that everything has a multiplier effect: If it is well-managed, an entrepreneurial team has vastly increased financial capital, mental capital, and network contacts. More importantly, the team synergy of like minds can make a team's success go through the roof.

Beware the monster, however. Since complexity of management increases exponentially, not proportionally, anything less than true visionary leadership and total team commitment will result in bureaucracy or chaos.

Employees Few student businesses formally hire employees until business has a yearly cash flow of tens of thousands of dollars. However, informal "hiring" is commonplace. Employment divides up the work without giving up the control. It provides employment and personal or financial development to those not capable, or willing, or ready, for entrepreneurship. In my third year of Van's Services, I hired several employees part-time and one full-time. Since they were conscientious and committed, we had a fun and profitable season.

On a larger scale, having employees can mean immense profits. It also carries with it responsibilities that complicate management of your main activities, in addition to robbing you of all but a little academic and personal time. It can also mean such quagmires as liability insurance, Social Security taxes, federal employee taxes, and other concerns.

Independent contractors In the late '80s, networking has come into vogue, with entrepreneurs acting as independent contractors for one another. It is simple, flexible, and it avoids tax and bureaucratic diarrhea. I now use this method exclusively, as do most other student entrepreneurs. For example, Karl Edelmann sometimes hires out work on a piecework basis (20 cents for each part assembled and boxed) to workers outside the family; Scott Mize uses a cooperative office service. The only drawbacks are possible lack of continuity and the lack of a defined chain of command, which is often helpful for quick decision-making.

High-tech help   You may be able to meet your expansion needs perfectly by simply plugging into technology. Most student entrepreneurs use a computer for tasks that used to prevent all but the rich from entering business. For example, a simple bookkeeping program can save you just as much time and *much* more money than hiring an accountant; a word-processor can eliminate some secretarial chores you would have to farm out otherwise. You may have to make a substantial investment—in both money and time—when you first computerize your business. In most cases the increased efficiency is well worth it later on.

EVALUATING YOUR NEEDS

It doesn't matter how busy you are; it's possible that hiring more people can make you even busier, yet you still get less business done! To successfully leverage yourself, the only thing that counts is your ability to organize human resources toward productive goals and pay people well for their services. I learned this lesson the hard way.

In high school, I tried to hire a secretary to retype and submit my plays to publishers. The guy freaked out at the work and left in a couple of days. But I didn't learn my lesson until my sophomore year of college. I made a business plan. I made a budget. I figured I could pay a secretary $6 per hour on an independent contractor basis. I kept her busy with lots of little details, but not the kind of work that paid the bills. After four weeks with little true accomplishment, I ran out of the cash needed to give her regular hours and she was ready to quit.

The final straw came one Monday morning the week of my midterm exams. I woke up at 10 A.M. that morning and got set to work. I realized Susan wasn't there, so I called her up and angrily asked, "Well? Where are you?" She responded, "I arrived at 8 A.M. just like I promised. The question is, where were you?"

She quit that minute. I went into a funk and didn't hire anyone again for months. All my Dad had to say was, "I thought it was the biggest mistake you ever made in your business. You were wasting not only your own money, but the money we set aside for college. I had to bite my tongue

CALLAHAN

"You're not here, Wilson—I like that in an employee."

on that one, but I kept my peace because I knew you had to learn it on your own."

To evaluate your needs for hired or other help, consider your current budget. How much money is coming in? How much of that is profit? More importantly, how much would be coming in if hired help gave you extra productivity? Since it's impossible to know these things in advance, especially your first time in business, talk to your parents and other experienced student entrepreneurs for help—and don't be afraid to proceed by the seat of your pants.

As you define your needs, distinct roles should emerge, such as, "I need someone to answer phones and organize my paperwork." Or, "I need a partner to share capital and risks with." Make a job description on paper. Once you know your needs exactly, start looking.

Teaming up with friends and family is a tricky issue. While many experienced entrepreneurs feel they ruined friendships by going into business together, the fact is that almost any partnership of student entrepreneurs you look at was started by roommates, or friends, or brothers and sisters. A surprising number of relationships actually get *better* through business.

The way I see it, if a friendship is so brittle that it would be destroyed by the stresses of business, neither the friendship nor the friend's interpersonal business skills are very good in the first place. The only thing that counts is: Does the other person have the skills and commitment for a team success? If an outsider has the skills and commitment, great. You can find such people through entrepreneurs' clubs and the entrepreneurial grapevine. But if friends or family have the skills and commitment, so much the better. Consider these questions:

Choosing a Compatible Business Partner

Do his or her strengths complement your weaknesses?

Does he or she have a history of success? Of being dependable?

Is he or she an open, frank communicator? Or is she/he gratingly direct, or wishy-washy?

Are your goals congruent? Could they be mutually shaped to be that way?

Are your personalities compatible? Would he or she be fun to work with?

Do his or her references show success-oriented qualities and accomplishments? Or are they vaguely positive recommendations—which usually are B.S.?

What is your gut feeling?

It would be ideal to have defined your needs and policies clearly before you bring other people on board. If you have enough foresight to create procedures for handling hours, payroll, quality control, etc., in advance, go for it. The reality is that everything is up in the air in a new business. Procedures may have to be worked out as you go along. Start with a few guidelines and go from there. The basic strategy is to keep the lines of communication open and to stay flexible.

THE NEW MANAGEMENT SCHOOL

Flexibility is a key idea from the New Management School—one of the most rapidly growing "schools" in America. But don't try to look up the address of the admissions office. If you go looking for the professors you'll find only a handful of articulate writers like Peter Drucker, Thomas Peters and Robert Waterman, Kenneth Blanchard, Marilyn Ferguson, and John Naisbitt. If you search for the student body, you'll find countless more people that have arrived at the same common-sense ideas. They have been sensible for centuries, but are only now starting to become common: ideas like personal responsibility, win/win negotiating, synergistic teamwork, and intensive communication.

Scott Mize gives an example. "The assumption of New Age Business is that if you give people control and input into their jobs rather than dictating to them, they are going to better know (and do) their jobs. People are responsible and creative and will work best if left alone, as opposed to beating them with a whip."

Student entrepreneurs have been among the first to pick up these ideas and make them standard business practice. It's been easy, because our generation never had to unlearn the "dog-eat-dog" paradigm, dismantle rigid hierarchies, or reprogram knee-jerk prejudices. One student entrepreneur confesses, "We don't know the rules. Nobody told us we're not supposed to do this or that. That accounts for a lot of our success."

Intensive communication   In small entrepreneurial companies, communication is easy and spontaneous. Whether they go between partners or "network nodes" (individuals communicating within a network), ideas cross like electric current. Through deliberate or informal brainstorming, new ideas are conceived, problems are worked out, and flexible procedures are put in place. Our youth orientation and informality bring out ideas that smoke-filled boardrooms and stuffy business suits kill.

Some practical ideas for stimulating communication include:

1. Keep the channels of communication open. Use "management by agreement" to mutually decide on plans, policies, and how to handle screw-ups.

2. Have a regular time for brainstorming ideas with co-workers and other entrepreneurs. Entrepreneurs' clubs are perfect for this.

3. Use your contacts to stay aware of everything that is going on.

4. Always follow up. Nobody ever does anything until he or she is reminded three times, and people often forget crucially important things—especially promises made over the phone. Don't fret about flaky people. Just adapt to human nature and take responsibility for calling people, even though they said, "I'll call you back."

Personal responsibility We all have a caged eagle inside us that, once freed, never can return to the gilded cage. Today, many people are experiencing such freedom. They never can go back to rigid, authoritarian structures in any arena of life—especially bureaucratic, unfulfilling jobs. In business, the young entrepreneurs are leading the way. They structure their companies so that co-workers are interdependent yet highly autonomous. They encourage personal responsibility stemming from a sense of ownership in the company. (Or actual ownership: See "Win/win," below.)

"Delegation" is an old-fashioned word, left over from hierarchical, authoritarian models of kingdoms, regimes, and empires. Today it is being replaced by "self-management." Instead of having to tell someone to pick up a piece of litter, tighten a bolt, or otherwise delegate duties, the new managers create an atmosphere where co-workers assign themselves tasks in their areas. One of the most influential management ideas of the '80s was the concept of *The One Minute Manager*, as articulated by Kenneth Blanchard and Spencer Johnson. The concept is ingenious. *Have co-workers write down their daily goal and plan for achieving it.* It can be as easy as writing goals down on a notecard, and it often does only take one minute. Your only task as a manager is to facilitate their actions and keep them focused on the task. We used this technique in ACE at UCSD and were successful. (The key, we learned, after mutually blowing it a couple of times, is *followup*, which takes far more than "one minute"!)

Some action ideas:

1. Try task cards. If someone at an ACE at UCSD brainstorming session volunteered to paint a banner or check out a potential enterprise, I asked him or her to make a 3 × 5 "task card" on it. He or she would write down the self-assigned goal, the how-to plan, and the deadline on a note card. This adaptation of the "one minute manager" can be used between partners, independent contractors, or even several entrepreneurs who are doing business together.

2. Trust them! Once a task has been farmed out, give the person free rein in that area. Inexperienced people will need more guidance, but the best way to develop their skills is by allowing them the space to make mistakes—as long as they don't cause harm to your overall product quality. In my lawn care and window washing businesses, my partners and I quickly worked out an agreement: We would honor each other's decisions.

Win/win Frisbee has always been my favorite game. There are no winners or losers. If you throw the Frisbee well and make it easy to do my special double-handed-under-the-crotch-snatch then we both win (this is a difficult move that looks as obscene as it sounds). But if you throw my cherished Aerobie in the ocean and it sinks, we both lose. And I might toss you in after it!

The concept of the double win is one of the most valuable ideas of our time, and it has been articulated well by my former employer, Dr. Denis Waitley, in his book, *The Double Win*. In its precursor, the best-selling audiocassette album *The Psychology of Winning*, he says the double win means "If I help you win, then I win, too."

"Win/win" also has to do with making a contribution to the larger society in which we live. Brett Kingstone has made it a point to hire Viet Nam vets, many of them severely handicapped, in his companies.

Here are some action ideas to help you achieve win/win in business:

1. Offer incentives, bonuses, and other profit-sharing plans to employees, if you have them.

2. Praise people. Laurie Stewart makes this a key part of her speeches to businesses. She believes, "Make people feel special and they'll give their very best."

3. Pay on a piecework basis, where possible. Studies in psychology show that an immediate reward proportional to the work done results in the highest productivity. When I was running Van's Services, I found my co-workers were far more motivated when I paid them by the lawn, instead of by the hour.

4. Play win/win with everyone. Karl Edelmann says the pricing policy of Edelkinder GMBH is, "We leave enough

on the table so everyone gets a fair share. In other words, we don't price our parts so that we don't make any money, but we also don't price the part so that the buyer or middle man can't make any money either."

Synergy Synergy is the essence of teamwork. It literally means having a product that is greater than the sum of its parts. In practice, it is teamwork, pure and simple. Teams can get things done that individuals simply can't do. In innovative young companies, committed teams are accomplishing things that old hierarchical companies never could.

For example, many U.S. companies are beginning to borrow the Japanese practice of quality control circles. These are groups of co-workers who literally get together in circles to discuss problems and propose solutions. When facilitated properly, these groups produce tremendous creativity and group morale. *That's* synergy.

Here are some action ideas for creating synergy:

1. Hold a brainstorming session with co-workers or other entrepreneurs. There is simply no better demonstration of synergy in action.

2. When possible, work side by side. Take turns instead of delegating the "peon work" to the lowest person on the totem pole. In Van's Services, if there was manure to be shoveled, we all did it, from the hired man to the company president. Sometimes we sang as we worked. (I think at that moment we were singing Lynyrd Skynyrd's "That Smell . . . ")

CREATING THE TEAM

No one starts out perfect—far from it. Companies are finally learning today that it's much more resourceful (i.e.,

*"When I told you guys to stagger your lunch hour
this isn't exactly what I had in mind!"*

better for the bottom line) to retrain and develop employees rather than fire them and have to search for new ones. Dan Bienenfeld, who has 183 sales representatives, says, "Promote from within. You can't teach a newcomer the industry without a lot of effort."

No matter what kind of team you put together, there are many cost-effective ways to motivate and train them, such as books, tapes, and seminars. Although the benefits tend to be long-term, there are short-term ones as well, such as a newly inspired employee's drive to double sales this week. Even if you don't have partners or employees *per se*, your "team" consists of those you do business with. The people I do business with help each other by exchanging motivational books and tapes, and several of my friends decided to go into business after I helped them get to the ACE convention.

Ultimately, the best way to build a team is to lead by example. You can't expect other people to grow unless you are growing yourself! (See Chapter 12.) It takes total commitment, integrity, and enthusiasm to fire up anyone you work with. Scott Mize sums it up: "People are more than just boxes on an organizational chart. The stereotype of Western business is, 'Who cares about people's feelings?—The bottom line is profit.' That's not New Age business. What we need to create for people is a better quality of life. It's going to make them more creative and give them something they want to work for."

11

THE BUSINESS PHYSICIAN'S DESK REFERENCE

What to Do When Your Business Gets a Cold

"Every generation needs a new revolution."
—Thomas Jefferson

ON-LINE ADVENTURE

featuring
David Fogel of Hotline Software

"You can almost hear the clop-clop on the cobblestones as the hansom carriage pulls away. . . . The safety of the citizens of Victorian London rests solely in your hands as you examine the facts, identify important clues, and uncover the truth . . . as Sherlock Holmes."

Writing press releases is only one of the many talents of 22-year-old David Fogel. He also composes music, flies airplanes, writes books, and creates computer software.

His first major program, "Holmes," was the product of 500 hours' work. Every detail is impeccably British (some "constables" know "alehouses" a little better than they should). David explains, "The key to making a text adventure is to make it as real-life as possible . . . it's not like TV shows or video games where you're bombarded with preconceived images; it's more like the old radio shows where *you* have to do the thinking."

A large part of writing anything with lasting appeal is refining and debugging your prose before it goes to market. David remarks, "In software writing, the measure of quality lies in the quality of your logic. I've gone through other mystery games and come up with different, but equally plausible, solutions to the mysteries. That better not happen in mine!"

David's press releases on "Holmes" and Hotline Software helped him get publicity in *USA Today* and Apple Computer's *inCider* magazine. He smiles knowingly, "A little self-promotion can be a very positive thing. The media depend on you for information." Finding a publisher was a little more difficult. It took 42 rejections before he found two publishers who market the program for 8 to 10 percent royalties. Data Command sells one version to schools for $50 and Artworks sells a different version to the public for $9.

Next, David put his writing skills to work on a book. Since he was studying statistics at the University of California, Santa Barbara, he submitted a proposal to his professors to do an independent study on horse racing statistics. His research led to a book, *The Mathematics of Horse Racing*, which will be published in the fall of 1988 by Liberty Publishing Co.

On weekends, David works for a research and development company. They have given him free rein to develop an evolution-based model for artificial intelligence. "Basically what I'm doing is teaching the computer how to learn on its own. It proposes alternative logics and chooses the best one, and that serves as the parent generation for the next." Sherlock himself would doff his double duck-billed bonnet in admiration. The work is so engaging that despite the proximity of San Diego's beach and glistening sun-worshippers, he rarely can be found lounging. He grins, "I hate to be unproductive!"

Once upon a time, at a ritzy snobbish college, there was a young man named Clyde Dumlutz who came into some big money. His rich uncle, who had built a successful development firm, left him $10,000 so that he, too, could be an entrepreneurial success. Clyde had heard that being an entrepreneur was sexy, so he thought he'd give it a whirl. Besides, he figured he could write off all his college expenses and go to fancy business luncheons all the time. And heck, with no bosses, he could work any old hours he wanted. Or hardly at all.

After several weeks of perusing the glossy ads showing what he was going to buy with all his profits, he finally had to decide what kind of business he would start. Suddenly he remembered an old drinking buddy who bragged about having international business contacts and decided to give him a call. Well, he swung a pretty hard bargain and got a truckload of slightly damaged E.T. T-shirts wholesale from Tijuana. Clyde reasoned that they would be a big hit with the geriatric crowd because E.T. looked so decrepit himself. He hired the most expensive ad agency in town to create an ad campaign around the theme "Wrinkles Is Beautiful."

After several weeks of waiting for someone to respond to his flyers and ads in the "Personals" section of *Old Folks Fashion Weekly*, his first order came in. He was so ecstatic he decided to go in debt to hit a larger section of the market. He persuaded his grandmother to star in a local TV ad and promised to make her vice president of international telemarketing as soon as he got his WATS line.

By now, Clyde had sold his motorcycle and was almost out of cash. Unpaid bills were piling up, his Basic Accounting 101 homework remained undone, and his underwear was beginning to smell. His only customer, after discovering the bullet hole and the stain under the right armpit, returned the only T-shirt he had sold. Then came the straw that broke the camel's back: His grandmother went on strike.

Clyde himself may not exist, but there have been real business failures that would make him look like a financial prude. In San Diego, a miserable little shyster named J. David Dominelli frittered away the better part of $180 million of investors' money for "business expenses" (like a 2-million-dollar mansion) in a business that didn't even exist. He's in prison now. Pity.

Although this book has promoted the benefits and good times involved in entrepreneurship, there's something else you ought to know. It ain't all fun 'n' games. You *could* lose money. Your grades *could* drop. (They probably will, at first.) And your grandmother *could* even go on strike.

Business problems like these, arising from poor decisions and neglect, are just like diseases in the human body: They make you feel awful, they sap up all your money and energy, and they can lead to complications and even to the death of your business.

The following Business Physician's Desk Reference is concerned with recognizing, treating, and especially preventing three types of business diseases:

Mental disorders (poor planning);

Communicable diseases (communication problems);

Ruptures and dysfunctions (lack of quality control).

The diseases can lead to complications, which really do occur in business because big problems usually start out as little ones. While the terms in this chapter are only used metaphorically, physical ill health actually can result from managing your affairs poorly. Ulcers aren't so much a result of what you're eating, but what's eating you.

NINE DISEASES COMMON TO STUDENT BUSINESSES

1. Diminished Libido (Lack of the Creative Urge)

Symptoms: Inability to think of new ideas or new ways to market products; inability to adapt to new situations.

Acute complications: Impotence from repeated failure to succeed; desire to get out of business altogether (suicide).

Case History: This disease is extremely rare among student entrepreneurs, who are by nature still very creative and excited about the new possibilities ahead of them. But we have a well-known example in our culture: Chrysler Corporation's failure to give the public what they wanted left it in the dust behind more innovative companies. Luckily the combined forces of teamwork, Lee Iacocca, and a loan guaranteed by Uncle Sam turned it around.

Rx: Survival for entrepreneurs requires constant innovation. Stimulate your entrepreneurial creativity by associating with other like-minded people and keeping your eyes open to unfilled market needs. If the problem persists, take two sheets of paper, fill them up with brainstorming ideas, and call a business doctor in the morning.

2. Deafness (Insensitivity to Market Needs)

Symptoms: Inability to listen to what people need; failure to sell unmarketable items and services.

Acute complications: Malnutrition from inadequate business income; bruises from failing to hear warnings about obstacles in your path.

Case History: According to one expert that many call a true "business doctor," Dr. James Belasco, the number-one reason companies fail is that they get out of step with what people really want. The entrepreneurs who fall in love with the product itself—and lose sight of their customers' needs—eventually fail. One example is Beth Whiting.

Beth's business was going great. She could hardly fill her orders for handmade jewelry. One item was especially hot: hair barrettes made out of colorful beads. Every fashion-conscious sixth-grader wanted one to make the scene. So Beth ordered 96,000 beads from Germany, thinking she could profit from such an economy of scale. As it turned out, the sixth-graders' fickle passions turned to other novelties, and Beth was left with 80,000 beads rolling around in her basement.

Rx: The healing powers of the earth are miraculous. Just keep your ear to the ground and you'll be able to follow market trends with ease. Specifically, conduct a simple survey of your fellow students or whoever you will be selling to, and/or test-market samples of your product before you spend a lot of money. And do as Mama always wanted: Clean the wax out of your ears.

3. Nearsightedness (Lack of Foresight and Good Planning)
Symptoms: Inability to focus on priorities; failure to see the big picture and stay on target.

Acute complications: Bulimia from poor budgeting of money intake and outgo; stunted growth from missing key opportunities.

Case History: This disease reaches nearly epidemic proportions among the new in business, producing a high infant mortality rate. We students are notoriously unable to structure our time and we have a million distractions all around us that keep us from focusing on our priorities. As a result, only a few student entrepreneurs ever reach their full potential. An example of a good recovery is David Fogel.

When David arrived at college, there were too many things to do and not enough time to do them. The former valedictorian's freshman grades looked like a Scrabble hand that could spell CuCCoo. Both his grades and his spirits picked up when he learned how to set his priorities within a college context. He then succeeded in writing his labyrinthian murder mystery software, "Holmes," and a book on rational gambling as well.

Rx: Keep asking yourself: "What business am I really in?" "What's most important to accomplish this year? This month? Today? Right now?" Write down your goals, prioritize them, and slot them into your calendar or organizer. David says, "You need to admit what you are doing wrong and change it."

4. Paralysis (Procrastination; Lack of Followup)
Symptoms: Bills piling up and overflowing the "in" box; deadlines flying by; an untapped file of business contacts never followed up.

Acute complications: Inflammations from irritated customers and suppliers who complain about slow payments; broken heart from missed opportunities.

Case History: It was blowin' like the devil's breath itself and Marc Magor was out having a hell of a time. Flying along the dunes of Lake Michigan in his hang glider, he came to a jetty. In order to get around it, he had to fly over the water. Once he got out there, he realized he was losing altitude *fast*. By the time he finally decided to turn back toward land, it was too late. The wind forced him to make a downwind "landing" in deep water. Marc recalls, "I saw my life flash before my eyes. I was about to be trapped underwater, underneath the wing. I knew I was a goner." Just then, a gust of wind flipped the whole thing pilot-side-up, allowing him to untangle himself from his harness straps and swim to shore. "I know Someone or Something was looking out for me that day," swears Marc, "but I'll never put off a decision again!"

Rx: If it's getting hard to get yourself in motion, maybe you should sit on a sharp tack. Always follow up any business lead, verbal agreement, or letter *immediately*. The call or letter doesn't need to be long—just do it!

5. Asthma (Allergic Reaction to Promotion and Publicity)

Symptoms: Paleness from lack of exposure and aversion to the very media that could help the business take off.

Acute complications: Xenophobia, or fear of strangers, from not promoting yourself enough to attract new customers.

Case History: Ken Appel and his friends at UCSD's KB Books started out selling discount textbooks from the trunk of Ken's car. No one knew about them. But once the school paper did a cover story on the project, sales took off and they opened a regular store.

Rx: Put shyness in the closet where it belongs and promote yourself. Remember, you are unique and certain media want you very badly, so seek them out.

6. Amnesia (Poor Recordkeeping)

Symptoms: Slipped disks from losing your computer data; jangled nerves from unexpected bills popping up.

Acute complications: Blood loss from forgotten accounts receivable; dislocated shoulder from having your arm twisted to pay old bills.

Case History: As a first-time author with an almost evangelical zeal for people to read my book, *High School Superstars*, I loaned the books out willy-nilly or said "pay me later." I'm now convinced that those three words don't enter the brain verbatim, but are garbled en route to mean "no charge." Because I forgot to record some of the amounts owed me, much of the money will never be recovered.

Rx: Bookkeeping isn't that hard; you just have to keep on top of it. Set a regular time each day or week to record income and expenses in an organized ledger or computer system, and keep a receipt for each item sold.

7. Anemia (Poor Cash Flow)

Symptoms: Stunted growth from undercapitalization; disfigurement from not being able to present a good image.

Acute complications: Loss of strength if employees leave because they're not paid well enough or regularly enough; paralysis if there is no money to buy new equipment or inventory.

"It hurts when I go like this!"

Case History: Dan Bienenfeld's tale probably sounds familiar to emerging entrepreneurs: "We were applying for a loan from the Small Business Administration and also needed a letter of credit from our bank. Then we got turned down by the bank and on our SBA loan, but our printer in Hong Kong had already gone to press. Our company was going to fold one way or the other. Even if we got the money, but it was two weeks late, we'd lose hundreds of thousands of dollars in orders. So, what we did was go to the printing company and paint the picture for the people there. We worked out a deal with the company directly, and got the calendars out on time."

Rx: Often shoestringing (reinvesting profits) just won't allow you to grow fast enough to justify working for yourself.

Be sure to get enough money at the start to keep things running until your business can generate enough income to sustain itself, and always keep a financial cushion in the bank to get you through lean times.

8. Hyperactive Exhaustion (Quality Control Problems)

Symptoms: Breathlessness from doing too many things at once; cuts and bruises from making careless mistakes.

Acute complications: Muscular atrophy from negligence, causing equipment failure and customer complaints; ulcers from guilt over screw-ups.

Case History: During the third year of operating my high school lawn service, I began to get real cocky. I had this idea that every 60 seconds was worth 15.6 cents, so I began rushing around like a robot gone haywire. I sprinted behind the lawn mower, trimmed hedges at a hasty clip, and raced my truck between jobs. Pretty soon people began to complain about streaks in their lawns.

Reality didn't sink in until the flashing red light appeared in the rearview mirror. The cop pulled me over and strode up to my car.

"Young man," she demanded, "do you have any idea how long I've been following you?"

"Uh, well you see, um, there's this big mound of grass blocking my view, and um—"

"Or any idea how fast you were going?"

"A tad over the limit?"

"Fifty-two miles an hour. This is not the Indy 500, young man. It's a school zone!"

Rx: Quality starts with your own sense of integrity. How do you want to feel about your product or service? How much do you care about your customers? And by all means, *never* let counting minutes interfere with quality control. If you're an entrepreneur, think like an entrepreneur, not like a minimum wage worker! Don't watch the clock. Watch the results you're producing.

9. Osteoporosis (Lack of Support)

Symptoms: Brittle ego; bruises from falling down over and over again.

Acute complications: Burnout; identity crises

Case History: As an entrepreneur, you're right on the cutting edge of the highest highs. You're also under the wheel of the lowest lows. As an author/entrepreneur, I've felt very lonely at times. In quiet moments, sitting alone at my typewriter, my only companion is an evergreen swaying in the wind outside my window. I mutter to it, "I wonder what a 'normal' job would be like?"

And even if you're physically surrounded by people, you can still feel isolated. Some of it has to do with other people's miseducation about business. Many have this idea that profit is somehow "evil." They look at you as if you were from another planet. Some of the isolated feeling comes from within—from not being able to relate to people who are not positive thinkers. How can a high-energy, global-minded entrepreneur relate to someone whose big thrill in life is drugging his mind with sitcoms or his body with chemicals?

Rx: Entrepreneurship may be independent, but it doesn't have to be lonely. Associate with other entrepreneurs—and better yet, form or be part of a team of committed individuals all working for the same goal together. You can pool money and resources, divide the labor according to time and talents, and especially keep each other motivated.

Laurie Stewart uses teamwork to stay motivated: "I recently got together with a friend and we put our goals on paper. We signed and dated it and promised we'd keep reminding each other. She calls me every week to see how I'm doing on it."

PREVENTIVE MEDICINE

It may seem like a legion of illnesses threatens to descend if you even think about starting your own small business. Don't panic. These metaphorical ills will stay far away with good management practices. Prevention of each one of them falls into one of three categories:

Ideas

People

Things.

Ideas problems in business are your natural strength as an entrepreneur. A steady diet of thought-provoking reading material and mental exercise with entrepreneur-minded friends will keep you bubbling over with innovative ideas.

People problems will rarely arise if you put the majority of your time into serving your customers and building a good business team. A big smile and a sincere interest in people will yield unforeseen dividends in referral business, contacts, and good will.

Equipment failure and other things problems belong to careless people, not you. You ultimately are responsible for your success. Keep a close watch on your quality control, bookkeeping, cash flow, and equipment maintenance. Stay on top of debts and deadlines. No one cares how fast you do the job—just how well you do it.

12
TIME FLIES —FLY WITH IT!
Time Management and Motivation

"The journey *is* the destination."
–Theme of Apple Computer, Inc.

SPEAKING FROM THE HEART

featuring
Laurie Stewart of L. A. Stewart Productions

Laurie Stewart, a 26-year-old professional speaker, quips, "They say that the number one fear people have is public speaking. Number two is the fear of death. That means most people would rather die than speak in public!"

Laurie herself takes on that fear boldly, speaking to groups all over the United States about interpersonal communication, goal setting, and personal growth. She recently graduated from Western Michigan University in Kalamazoo, Michigan, where she studied marketing and communications. It was there that she got so turned on to public speaking that she decided to found an organization on campus called S.P.E.A.C.—Speaking for Pleasure, Experience, Arts, and Challenge. Through that organization, she discovered she had a marketable talent that could bring her fulfillment and income, so she started preparing to speak professionally.

Like every speaker from Norman Vincent Peale to Paul Harvey, she stumbled at first. She recalls, "When I gave a speech, it felt like my stomach had a bowling ball in it. I couldn't even get my voice out of my throat."

Rapid improvement came when she sought out a professional speaker to teach her the poise and perils of the platform. She found Bill Sanders, of whom she says, "He helped me more than he'll ever know." He taught her everything he knew, from how to size up an audience to how to recover from a bad joke. His best advice, recalls Laurie, was "Pay your dues—get out there and speak every chance you get."

Laurie took his advice seriously, and gave over 50 speeches free of charge so she could build her reputation. If they still insisted on paying her, she turned it over to charity. She made a brochure and approached various groups such as fraternities and campus organizations, as well as area community and youth groups.

Four years after deciding to go pro, she is now sought out by groups from Arizona to Florida. Her fee is $750 plus expenses in-state, $1,000 plus expenses out-of-state. Her seminar for businesses, "Getting Your Life in Shape," focuses on the importance of first impressions, a healthy self-concept, and communication skills.

Her next goal is to become popular enough to charge $1,500 per speech and start hiring support people. It's clear she loves what she does. She confesses, "The motivation I had from my freshman speaking class and professional speech class has multiplied daily, monthly, and yearly. It's a passion, it's a desire, it's a flame inside me. I really feel God's spirit working through me. Speaking is a new opportunity to help people."

Time is irreplaceable. It is your single most important asset. No one could ever put an absolute value on it, because unlike money it can't be banked, traded, stolen, or even killed. It can only be managed. Managed efficiently, every hour can help make each of your dreams come true. The purpose of this chapter is to help you:

Clarify your goals;

Achieve your most important priorities;

Balance school and entrepreneurial activities;

Motivate and empower yourself.

Do you want to make $10,000 this year? Do you want to help people and serve their needs through your business? You can. The students featured in this book prove it's possible. They are successful because they have learned to effectively manage their time, their goals, and themselves. Since time management involves more than just managing each day, I will present a simple yet complete system for planning your goals, from the distant future to the present moment. I call it the "Sequence for Success."

THE SEQUENCE FOR SUCCESS

Every great business—from Celestial Seasonings to IBM—began as an idea in someone's mind.

From a Vision it became a Goal.

From a Goal it became a Plan.

From a Plan it became a Schedule.

From a Schedule it became Action.

From Action it became Followup.

From all these things, the Dream became a Reality.

This is the basic Sequence for Success I teach in my leadership and goal-setting seminars. Although most people only talk about goal setting in isolated, abstract terms, I'm convinced it's the *whole* process that gets results. To illustrate how the process works, I'll discuss how to do each part in terms of writing a book.

Daydreaming   The ability to conceive innovative, feasible ideas is what sets entrepreneurs apart from mere managers. Your success as an entrepreneur depends on your creative ideas. Although creativity can't be *learned* with some cookbook-style formula, it can be *developed* by exposing yourself to many ideas. Read, attend seminars, and exchange ideas with creative, open-minded people. Your creativity also can be sharpened by practice. Two applied techniques are brainstorming and visualizing.

Brainstorming is fun and generates vast numbers of ideas. It's simple: just write down as many ideas as you can without stopping. Evaluate them only after you have written them all down. Never stop yourself from including what seems like a silly idea, because it might lead to a not-so-silly one.

Visualizing involves vividly seeing the realization of your dreams. These are few mental techniques as important to an entrepreneur as visualization. Dr. Denis Waitley, motivational psychologist for the U.S. Olympic team, the Apollo astronauts, and many Fortune 500 companies, has proven that having a clear picture of your intended outcome will automatically direct your subconscious mind to do whatever is necessary to make it a reality.

Laurie Stewart, who is sought after for her presentations on goal setting and positive attitudes, uses visualization at least five minutes a day. She notes: "I see myself presenting a speech in front of 5,000 people in a large auditorium. I see myself being humorous, becoming the best speaker I can be. I see them laughing and crying and enjoying themselves and my presentation. I see myself ending the speech and having them come up to me to ask how they can improve their lives."

To use visualization in your Sequence for Success, start with a brilliant, but yet-to-be-developed, idea you've generated through brainstorming or simple inspiration. (Creative ideas often come at the craziest times: shaving, showering, washing dishes.) See the ideal end result in your mind in vivid detail, including all the colors, sights, and sounds that would be there (and *will* be there). Next, see it developing over time, backward from the finished product to the initial idea.

For example, I visualized a book with an attractive cover selling madly at the Bookman bookstore in Grand Haven, Michigan (the specifics). Then I pictured submitting the manuscript to a publisher, then getting a contract, then making the outline for the book, then coming up with the idea in the first place.

The reason for "thinking backward" is that having an end result in your mind actually stimulates the creative, resourceful parts of your brain to come up with whatever is needed to accomplish each step. Marc Magor concludes, "Visualization is how things get done. It's just like hang gliding. If you can conceptualize it, you can achieve it."

Goal setting   A goal is simply a written statement of what you plan to accomplish. If you've visualized your goal, writing it down should be a cinch. Goals deal with end results, not with the process of getting there. (That is planning.) Make sure your business goals are:

1. Specific
2. Realistic
3. Measurable
4. Dated.

Here is an example: "I commit to write a 180-page book, *Excelling: High School Superstars and How to Be One*, and submit it to Rosen Publishing Group in New York by February 1, 1984."

Or it could be as simple as, "My goal this week is to make ten sales, yielding a profit of $200."

Planning Planning is the systematic breakdown of a goal into bite-sized pieces. Plans are activities that can be put on a things-to-do list. To plan effectively, recall your visualization. What tasks need to be done to achieve your outcome? What order must they be done in? What smaller tasks need to be done to accomplish the larger tasks? My plans for writing my book included:

1. Find someone to help revise the manuscript by October 12.
2. Write two sample chapters and an outline by July 1.
3. Write to ten New York publishing houses by July 1.
4. Learn to use my word processor by April 20.

Prioritizing Ever felt like you were going in a million directions at once? Involved in a dozen projects, of which half were destined to be left unfinished? A typical entrepreneur will be faced with a hundred possible things to do at any given time. The most successful ones give first priority to the items that yield the biggest payoff. By acting early on deadlines, they don't spend as much time and worry putting out fires later.

In his book and in a personal interview, time management expert Merrill Douglass underlined the distinction between "important" activities and "urgent" activities. He suggested that those goals and activities that bring the best *results* should be done first, as opposed to doing the least-stressful ones first, which results in "busyness" but not success.

When prioritizing your goals or plans, ask yourself: "What long-term benefit will this action bring me, compared to other items? What would happen if I didn't do it?"

Scheduling   A plan that is scheduled gets done. Take your plans and priorities and put them on your calendar or daily to-do list. If you would put a dentist appointment on your calendar, why not put your goals there, too? Isn't achieving your life dream as important as routine hygienic chores?

Be sure to leave large allowances for potential setbacks and interruptions. Don't worry about following your schedule perfectly; something more immediate might come up. Just shuffle and rearrange your schedule into blocks of time. The key is committing to make a schedule in the first place.

The Sequence for Success, with all its fancy-sounding techniques, really isn't complicated. Once you learn how to do it, it will take only a couple of minutes to organize each day in the morning, and perhaps as much as an hour or two once a week (say, Sunday evening) to organize the coming week. A time management planner can help structure these activities.

Time management planners   College means crazy schedules. Phone numbers scribbled on tiny scraps of paper just don't cut it if you want to get a lot done. A good calendar and address book are a start, but to really apply the Sequence for Success you need a system that allows you to plot out your plans from the idea stage down to up-to-the-hour schedules.

The best system I've run across so far is the Dayrunner system. It is a compact notebook with sections for idea development, goals, daily plans, progress charts, telephone numbers, a calendar, and a daily to-do list. It also has space for addresses and telephone numbers, business cards, and a checkbook. The Dayrunner currently costs $49 and it pays for itself within a week in extra productivity and peace of mind. In addition, carry a 3 × 5 card and a pen with you at all times. You never know when that million-dollar idea is going to hit you.

Larry Vein, a dynamic student entrepreneur from the University of Southern California, uses his Dayrunner every day and is being hired as an *intra*preneur (entrepreneur operating within someone else's business) by Dayrunner to develop and market "Campus Runner" for students. Watch for it.

It won't be long before lap computers replace notebooks. Several have built-in time management programs. Verne Harnish of ACE brings his lap computer everywhere. "It's great," he says. "All I need is a phone jack, and I can send and get something from my main computer at the office—no matter where in the world I am."

Getting it done   So many opportunities! So little time! Entrepreneurs typically have an abundance of energy, but many just barely scramble through each day. The one thing they lack is *focus*. Master the art of concentration, and there will be no project too ambitious, no problem too tough, no triathlon too long to complete. Two simple techniques can help you make concentrated use of your time: The $25,000 idea and time-block management.

The $25,000 idea   Professional speaker Bill Sanders shares this secret in "The Student's Guide to Earning Money." It is so valuable that one entrepreneur reportedly paid $25,000 for it. The story goes that years ago, a certain man boldly told millionaire Charles Schwab that he had an idea that would change his life. At first Schwab scoffed, but after the man insisted, he decided to listen to the idea and said, "I'll pay you whatever the idea is worth." The idea was simple, but it was so effective that Schwab paid him the $25,000. Here it is:

> Every day write down the six MOST IMPORTANT items you will do the next day, in the order you will do them.

The idea is so powerful because it helps you stay focused on *priorities*, not time-wasters. From a psychological standpoint, it is essential to write these items down the night before so that your subconscious will be working on the details while you sleep. If you're excited about your own goals and successes, you literally will be jumping out of bed the next morning to get cracking at those priorities.

Entrepreneurs tend to be morning people. Many student entrepreneur clubs schedule breakfast meetings because of this. The morning is the most productive part of the day, and you can get a lot of things done before the rest of the world even rubs the sleep out of its eyes. For me an ideal day begins at 6 A.M. with a run, bike ride, or swim where I preview the day ahead in my mind. These are my happiest, most productive days.

MANAGING BLOCKS OF TIME

Phone call. Visit. Snatch of studying. Pay bill. Phone call.
Fragmentation.

The interruptions never cease. How can you ever focus when your train of thought keeps being derailed? Chasing rabbits—that is, trying to handle details in a random, ramshackle fashion—is a stressful and unproductive habit. It can be eliminated by grouping related tasks together and accomplishing them in blocks of time. Phone calls, errands, bill-paying, bookkeeping, and making sales each can be grouped into blocks of time. For phone calls, choose one time each day to make them one after another. Put non-urgent letters in an "in" tray until you can respond to them all at once. Errands can be run once a week, and bill-paying can be done once or twice a month. Sticking to your blocks takes discipline, especially when circumstances upset your schedule. But isn't it worth it to have peace of mind and more control over your life?

*"I'll have two hamburgers, a small order of fries, and—oh.
Sorry, Sandy, it's been a confusing day."*

BALANCING SCHOOL AND BUSINESS ACTIVITIES

Student entrepreneurs are a hybrid product of two worlds. They are not quite full entrepreneurs, because they must devote part of their time to studies. They are not ordinary students either, since they face responsibilities and opportunities that never enter the consciousness of their peers. The double commitment creates a double bind when it comes to time management. While most choose work over school, a few successfully manage to keep their lives in balance. In fact, some find their grades *improving* because they're forced to study efficiently. To make sure you're allowing time for personal growth, block out plenty of time for school work, exercise, and a social life. Block-time for school and study will be totally devoted to those concerns alone, and business blocks will be devoted to business priorities. That way you won't feel guilty because you blew your calculus assignment by taking on yet another business commitment.

STAYING MOTIVATED

In Laurie Stewart's motivational seminars, she advises people to believe in their own potential, to think positive thoughts, and to set specific, dated goals. She advises, "Constantly feed your subconscious mind positive affirmations such as 'I am an intelligent person. I can do the job.' Tell them to yourself first thing when you get up in the morning, and also just before you go to bed."

It is a fact that your life will take the direction of your "currently dominant thoughts," according to Dr. Denis Waitley. People who spend most of their mental energy on despair and cynicism lose all resolve to make changes in their lives. They say things like "I'll never make it through this semester," or "What can one person do to change the system?" Entrepreneurs, on the other hand, often view the world in a constructively positive way. Since they think about their dreams all the time, they begin to manifest those dreams as realities in their lives.

To be truly successful, idealism needs to be tempered by realism. A truly successful entrepreneur is motivated by an ideal—a dream—and seeks to make it a reality by working out a real plan that takes into account all the real limitations of the real world. I call this kind of thinking "idrealism." I believe all successful dreamers are idrealists to some extent. They see things not as they *are*, but as how they *could be*. Their success depends greatly on the clarity of their vision: how well they see the end result and the means to achieve it.

"Clarity Is Power" is the slogan of millionaire Dwight O'Neill. He became wealthy by helping other people clarify their goals in a popular nationwide seminar, "Money and You." The key, says Dwight, is to know

what you want,

how to go about it,

and how to know whether you're getting it.

He recommends that you keep a scrapbook with photographs showing symbols of your goals. If you want a sports car, for example, cut out a photograph from a magazine of the exact car you want and look at it every day. One other millionaire I consulted for advice, Robert J. Sturner, put a picture of the Rolls-Royce he dreamed about on the sun visor when he was still driving an old car. He now drives the Rolls.

EMPOWERING HABITS FOR HIGH ACHIEVEMENT

You will find that staying concentrated on your goals gives you a power and energy that just isn't available to your listless peers who think it takes too much energy to get up and turn the knob on the TV set. Brett Kingstone quips, "If you *really* want to get something done, throw the TV out your window!"

Entrepreneurship requires a tremendous amount of energy. Research reveals that success is highly correlated with positive, preventive health habits. Many entrepreneurs exercise vigorously every day and eat only natural foods. Don Carruthers works out an hour a day and eats only healthful foods like fruit, cereals, and vegetables. He eats no meat, yet has a physique like Sylvester Stallone. Dan Bienenfeld also eats healthfully and swims at least one hour straight, every day. He says, "If you abuse your body, you're abusing your business as well as your personal life."

Being an entrepreneur gives you the space to work a lot on yourself. Entrepreneurs often make up the majority of the audiences at motivational seminars and they are typically hungry for self-improvement books and tapes. Appendix A lists many of these. The "Money and You" seminars are excellent, as are the seminars put on by the Small Business Administration (SBA). If you're serious about motivating yourself and those you work with, get plugged into the motivational tapes from Nightingale-Conant Corporation and SMI, Success Motivation Institute. They feature top motivators like Denis Waitley, Bill Sanders, Tom Peters, Ken Blanchard, and Zig Ziglar. Each product could be worth $25,000 in its own right.

This chapter has departed from some of the nuts and bolts of business and gone into the psychology of entrepreneurship for good reason: the success of your business rests mainly on your personal strengths, especially your use of time. The most important strengths, the ones that will make you a million dollars and help hundreds or thousands of people, are not in your bank account. They are located in your mind and in your character.

13

READIN' WRITIN' AND RETAIL

How to Integrate School and Entrepreneurship

"Entrepreneurs are the most potent revolutionary
force America furnishes to the world. . . . The
entrepreneur is the new non-violent change agent."
—Bob Schwartz
Founder, Tarrytown Executive House

HOT-WIRING REALITY

featuring
Brett Kingstone, Author

At age 28, Brett Kingstone has been recognized by
ACE as one of the top 20 entrepreneurs in the
nation under age 30, as well as one of the leading
spokespeople in the young entrepreneurs movement. His numerous businesses have produced
several million dollars in sales, and his book, *The
Student Entrepreneur's Guide*, has sold 150,000
copies. His example and his book helped convince
a generation of Americans that student entrepreneurship in the '80s is a reality to be respected and
encouraged.

Brett's first major enterprise began as an academic project at Stanford University. Encouraged
by his family, who were in the bedding business,
he chose to open a bedding company specializing
in electrically adjustable beds. He kept a display
model in a small showroom that he opened only
on Saturdays. The rest of the time he managed his
business from his dorm room and otherwise lived
the life of an (almost) ordinary student: studying
economics, practicing karate, and making decisions
in student government. Judging from a doodle in

the margin of the time planner picture in his book, he found time to chase girls as well.

As the Kingstone Bedding Warehouse project came to a close, Brett's advisor, Dr. Paul Griffin, put pressure on him to write not just the required project evaluation, but a book. Brett recalls the meeting vividly:

"Griffin sat back in his chair and said, 'No book, no grade.'

I stammered, 'You can't do that!'

'I can do anything,' he said smugly. 'I have tenure.' "

Brett set to work creating a top-notch book on how to start a part-time business during college. Besides elaborating on his own experience, he included short profiles of other successful student entrepreneurs with enterprises ranging from cookie-baking to multimillion-dollar franchises.

Through contacts and diligent searching, he found a willing publisher, McGraw-Hill. Brett also found an illustrator on his own campus, Gil Morales, whose character "Dupie" highlights each chapter. Brett was so impressed with Gil's potential that he helped him set up his own publishing company, Dupie Press, Inc.

The book was a phenomenal success. Brett was featured on the front page of the *Wall Street Journal*, in *Venture* magazine, and in his campus newspaper. He also appeared on the "Today" show.

After graduation, Brett became a full-scale entrepreneur. He traveled to Japan and the Soviet Union for business and education trips.

His next company, Gee Kee Fiber Optics, installed wiring for sophisticated exhibits at Disney World's Epcot Center and Disney Tokyo. He later started Kingstone-Prato. Brett explains, "Kingstone-Prato is an investment banking firm specializing in providing funding for young growing companies. We finance everything from fashion designers to aerospace defense contractors."

His latest project is writing another book, *The Dynamos: Who Are They Anyway?* It features 30 young and highly successful entrepreneurs under 30. Brett is confident of its potential and notes that reviewers have called it "The *In Search of Excellence* for the under-30 crowd."

Most students pay to study. A few get paid to study. That's what some clever student entrepreneurs are finding as they turn the tables on the system. By integrating their academic studies with their entrepreneurial pursuits, the information and skills they learn in class can help them succeed in business, and vice versa. In some cases, it happens the same day. Ken Appel was already in business by the time he decided to take his accounting courses seriously. He used his newly acquired knowledge to streamline his bookstore's recordkeeping system. Dan Bienenfeld created an 80-page business plan for several units of academic credit at UC Santa Barbara. The plan helped him acquire $80,000 in capital. And for all student entrepreneurs, academic expenses related to "professional development" are tax-deductible. Brett Kingstone legally wrote off a good part of his expenses at Stanford against profits from his Kingstone Bedding Warehouse.

Unfortunately, entrepreneurship and school don't always enjoy such a harmonious relationship. Student entrepreneurs typically report "being bored to death" by school, in Kim Merritt's words. She found that learning dry facts out of insipid textbooks was nothing like learning about chocolate and business at her own pace. Traditional schooling that puts the emphasis on passively learning information affects potential entrepreneurs more than it does any other type of student. What student entrepreneurs want is hands-on experience.

Entrepreneurship's frenetic, opportunity-driven pace and school's detail-oriented conformity potentially can split the attention of student entrepreneurs, as they have one foot in academia and the other in business. To escape almost literal schizophrenia, the "split-mind disease," they often drop out of school to pour more time into their business (many of the student entrepreneurs interviewed for this book left school for a semester, or in some cases more). While some never return, most do—but even then, they still don't feel part of the mainstream. David Goldman and his brother bemoaned the fact that when their business was just getting started, "Our social life dwindled and academics went out the door—we're looking forward to having a good time again."

I felt the split acutely during my first few years of college. I had this idea that being an entrepreneur in an academic setting was something to be ashamed of. I hid the fact that I was an author from all but my closest friends. I found my studies boring compared to entrepreneurial activities, and I doodled and daydreamed my way through an entire statistics course. I took a trimester off to concentrate on writing and entrepreneurial pursuits, but found myself neither doing these activities nor studying. I felt like a runny egg, sunny-side down.

Later, when I pulled it all together by my junior year, I felt I had succeeded in both school *and* my business.

The split doesn't have to last forever; in fact, it doesn't necessarily have to occur at all. There are several ways to integrate school and entrepreneurship:

ACADEMIC CREDIT

All student entrepreneurs agree that they learn much more through hands-on entrepreneurial experience than just from reading about it. Why not get academic credit at the same time? It may be easier than you think. In a business/economics curriculum, it should be easy to design an independent study plan like Dan Bienenfeld's business plan or Brett Kingstone's book. It can be done in virtually any major, from ceramics to computer science, and even psychology and English (see Appendix B).

If there's an established program such as independent study or a senior thesis project, you simply need to follow the guidelines. Where there is no path, however, use your entrepreneurial instincts to *create* one. The first step is to seek out a professor who you can convince of your sincerity. Working together, make a credible plan outlining the objectives of your project and how they will be measured. Be sure to indicate how it relates to your overall academic plans. Then submit the plan through the department to the proper authorities. Simple, right? Not quite. Be prepared to wade through impenetrable bureaucracies,

CALLAHAN

*"Of course things aren't always easy—Chuck being
on the road most of the time."*

endless lines, stacks of signatures, and other diabolical hassles. On the other hand, it can help you get those critical
credits needed to graduate.

ENTREPRENEURSHIP PROGRAMS

To play hardball with the big-league players, high-level yet
practical training is a must. Today over 250 universities
offer special programs geared to the needs of prospective
entrepreneurs, according to Dr. Karl Vesper of the University of Washington and author of *Entrepreneurship Education*. In an interview, he disclosed that today's programs
of study are much more complete than those of the late
'60s, when only a dozen or so universities offered courses

in entrepreneurship. He says the reason that entrepreneur programs are so popular is that "young people have always been impatient. They want to move ahead to new challenges and operate on their own initiative. The courses let them know what they need to acquire."

If you are seriously considering an undergraduate major in entrepreneurial studies or graduate work in this area, get your hands on Dr. Vesper's book. It is available through the Babson Center for Entrepreneurial Studies, Babson College, Wellesley, MA 02157.

OTHER TRAINING PROGRAMS

Seminars and support groups for entrepreneurs are plentiful. In any major city, there is bound to be an organization for entrepreneurs. Contact your chamber of commerce for leads.

One new trend in entrepreneurial training is "small business incubators." These are centers for aspiring entrepreneurs to share secretarial services, advertising and legal services, etc. In San Diego, Creative Systems Business Development, Inc., has devised a plan to pool the wits and capital of 50 first-time entrepreneurs. According to cofounder Tonya MacDonald, the group is planning weekly training seminars and brainstorming sessions. They hope their "small business incubator" will bring 50 healthy, bouncing businesses into the world without a single infant mortality.

The idea also is being tried in various parts of the country, and very likely in a city close to you. Again, check with your chamber of commerce or a business school department head, or even your local Small Business Administration office.

ACE—THE ASSOCIATION OF COLLEGIATE ENTREPRENEURS

There is no single more important resource for student entrepreneurs than ACE. Period. It offers exactly what a debutant entrepreneur needs: contacts. Verne Harnish, ACE's co-founder and recent director, says, "A young entrepreneur typically faces three major problems: a lack of business savvy, a lack of credibility, and lack of a well-developed network of contacts. ACE was formed to create a modern-day 'old-boy' network or 'young person network'."

ACE is only a few years old. It has grown from six members in 1983 to several thousand in 1988, representing several hundred universities and two dozen countries, including the People's Republic of China, Mexico, Australia, France, Great Britain, Canada, Japan, Spain, West Germany, Austria, Denmark, Brazil, Gambia, Korea, Thailand, and the Soviet Union! ACE offers quarterly newsletters, regional conferences, and an annual international conference. ACE has recently begun organizing business/pleasure trips for members to other countries, most notably, the People's Republic of China.

After attending two of the annual conferences, I can attest that today's ACE has more energy than tomorrow's fusion reactor. At the ACE convention in Los Angeles, 600 young entrepreneurs gathered to learn first-hand from entrepreneurial heroes like Steve Jobs. Student entrepreneurs such as Brett Kingstone and myself put on seminars and presented products and services at a half-day trade show. The partying and business card swapping went on 'til 3 A.M., and there were probably as many deals made as there were participants.

ACE's most practical value is in the affiliates that exist on many major college campuses. If your campus doesn't have one, start one!

ACE is also affiliated with YEO, the Young Entrepreneurs' Organization. If you're under 30 and have your own company, YEO offers the chance to network with your peers and serve as a speaker or advisor to undergraduate ACE groups. ACE and YEO can be contacted at:

> The Association
> of Collegiate Entrepreneurs
> Campus Box 147
> Wichita State University
> Wichita, KS 67208
> (316) 689-3000.

ENTREPRENEURIAL EDUCATION IN
PERSPECTIVE

Brett Kingstone, who has an excellent section on entrepreneurial education in his book, strongly feels, "I simply do not think you can learn entrepreneurship in college. In due respect to all the entrepreneurship programs across the country, they do not create entrepreneurs, no matter what they think. . . . For those who have the right kind of personality, I think the entrepreneurship programs serve a very important function in training them to learn from other people's mistakes and teaching them the basics of business: accounting, finance, management, for example."

In planning your studies, keep in mind the big picture. I feel it's vitally important to develop your *whole* self, of which your business acumen is just a part. College is too good to miss. When else would you ever give yourself the time and the freedom to decipher Shakespeare, learn how to write a coherent essay, or have the wild times and great friendships college can offer? Brett says, "Most importantly, in college I learned how to think."

Despite what some say, I believe it *is* possible to be a student entrepreneur and become well-educated and well-rounded at the same time. The key is figuring out *what* and *who* are most important in your life, and making time for them. Scott Mize makes time for study, travel, and good times and is still a top-flight entrepreneur as well. After returning to Harvard to finish his studies, he concluded, "I used to have a great sense of urgency. I wanted to go and make a million dollars right away. Now I believe there will still be opportunities when I get there."

START AN ENTREPRENEURS' CLUB

Every university and college should have an entrepreneurs' club. The benefits it can offer to students are much more current, focused, and relevant than a traditional student club. What do students at your school need? Money! An entrepreneurs' club can offer hundreds of ways to relate their studies to what they will practice out in the real world. An entrepreneurs' club can bridge that gap. And more than anything else, it offers entrepreneurial synergy: the barrier-breaking teamwork possible only when people pool their unique talents, energies, and ideas.

Do you have the kind of time, energy, and responsibility it takes to start such a club? Trying to do it alone would not only be inadvisable, but impossible. But with some like-minded co-founders, it's as fun as a good Frisbee game. You will need, however, one totally committed person to be the "front-runner," someone who will huff and puff until the idea catches on. Below is the basic plan we followed to make ACE at UCSD a reality.

1. Present the idea to like-minded students. You probably already know some other student entrepreneurs operating on campus. For other leads, ask several of the economics or business professors, or ask some savvy students within the student government. Make a commitment to one another to *do whatever it takes* to make the club happen.

2. Get faculty and institutional support. Many profs would give their favorite piece of chalk to see students actually act on the ideas they present in class, so finding an advisor shouldn't be hard. Approach your prospects with a specific game plan.

3. Contact the national ACE office. It can send you the ACE Franchise Package, which is a detailed step-by-step plan for starting an ACE club. The cost is $15 and it is worth every penny. This manual will help get things rolling faster than learning through unnecessary mistakes. Why reinvent the wheel?

4. Contact ACE club officers at other universities. I got some of the best ideas for the club from students I met at the national ACE convention. You can get contacts to these clubs by calling the national ACE office at (316) 689-3000.

5. Hold a kickoff event. Bring in a dynamic speaker who will get people fired up about entrepreneurship. Plaster the campus with posters, bury it in flyers, and deluge it with newspaper and radio ads and personal contacts. At the meeting, infuse the crowd with your vision of what the possibilities are for such a club, and channel the enthusiasm toward an organizational meeting held only a few days later.

6. Hold an organizational meeting. Decide on the club's purpose, and assign a team of students to write a charter. (There is a sample one in the ACE Franchise Package.) Don't expect the whole structure to fall in place at once; it may take awhile to see who the really committed leaders are. My experience was that the members resisted any formal structure at all at first, but later implemented a few organizational procedures for the sake of practicality.

7. Plan activities. Motivated people like entrepreneurs are bound to make things happen. Popular events include:

Speaker meetings
An all-day entrepreneurship conference
Networking parties
Business brainstorming parties
How-to clinics
Off-campus events and conferences (like the ACE convention)
Creative fund-raising.

Ongoing functions can include peer counseling for starting a small business, keeping a library of motivational materials and business opportunities, maintaining an "Offered/Needed" bulletin board (possibly included in a data base that members can access), and having a mentor program where young entrepreneurs can learn the ropes from a professional in the field.

Some experience-tempered advice: More than once I found myself scrambling just before an event or meeting trying to handle details I should have done already, or given to volunteers, or followed up long ago.

1. Make every effort to present a cooperative, educational image to authorities. We were careful to emphasize that ACE at UCSD was a nonprofit educational network. We also assured authorities that our efforts as a club on campus would be limited to fund-raising for the club as a whole, not for individuals.

2. Allow more lead time on projects than you can possibly imagine needing, especially if something needs to be approved by the campus bureaucracy.

3. Consult others frequently for advice, especially your advisor and ACE presidents at other universities.

4. Save the beer and wine for *after* the meeting. One meeting we laughed and joked deep into the evening until we realized we had gotten absolutely nothing done. We looked at the culprit—an empty jug of vin rosé—looked at each other, and burst out laughing all over again.

14

SPACESHIP: Entrepreneurship
EARTH/ in the
DESTINATION: New Age
ENTERPRISE

"There are no passengers on Spaceship Earth.
Everybody's crew."
–Marshall McLuhan

NEW AGE NETWORKING

featuring
Scott Mize of Mize Technology Development

For Scott Mize, the $50 an hour he often makes as a technology consultant isn't the best thing about being a student entrepreneur. It's the experience of seeing how the business world works and how it should change.

For the Mulvane, Kansas native, studying engineering at Harvard and cross-registering at M.I.T. wasn't enough. Helping start the Harvard Space Research Group, the Harvard Entrepreneurs, and the Association of Collegiate Entrepreneurs didn't give him a taste of the "real world" he was looking for either. To broaden his education, he needed to leave the Ivory Tower.

Scott's first major enterprise, Strawberry Software, took root with three other partners and a handful of seed money. They developed commercial business applications software, including a specialized spreadsheet/database program for the advertising industry and a state-of-the-art "top view" appointment calendar for executives.

The challenges of starting a company were often

more exciting than attending classes at Harvard. "My outside activities were taking a lot of time away from my school work," he recalls. "When I told my parents I intended to take a semester off, they were shocked and distressed." He did it anyway.

He eventually left Strawberry Software to start Mize Technology Development, his consulting business. He made enough money to travel all over the U.S. and, in three years, reaped over $100,000.

Scott's current philosophy on earning money fits into a larger game plan. "The reason I originally wanted to be an entrepreneur," Scott says, "is that I didn't want to worry about how much things cost. When I was a freshman, it really bothered me to have to ask, 'I wonder if I can afford this pizza?' Now I believe that entrepreneurship is ultimately a quest to remove money as a constraint on personal creativity.

"Entrepreneurship can also be a tool for social change, and what we really need is enlightened leaders," Scott states. He believes that "business-people-philosophers" will be among the foremost agents for change in the coming decades. "Entrepreneurs should not only be fiscally accountable, but also ethically, morally, and socially accountable. One of the goals of a company should be to treat people it touches as whole people, not just factors of production. And on the average, companies that are socially responsible perform better."

Progress will be accelerated most rapidly, he feels, through enhanced communication. For young entrepreneurs probably the best forum for ideas and contacts is the Association of Collegiate Entrepreneurs (and its affiliate, the Young Entrepreneurs Organization), which Scott cofounded with Verne Harnish and others.

Networking has been a key ingredient of his success. He usually has more offers than he can handle. Many of these contacts are people he met at the Boston Computer Society and through the extracurricular activities that were affecting his school work in the first place. Other contacts he met on-line, via computer networks like CompuServe, Delphi, and the Meta Network. "Contacts are incredibly important for getting hired," he says emphatically. "There could be 20 other people who can do a technical job, but the one who is visible and marketed will get it."

Networking has also allowed him to be a catalytic agent in many new ventures, both profit and nonprofit. He recently helped found an interdisciplinary higher education organization for the information age, the International Space University Project.

Although he lacks a fancy title and a brass plate on his door, Scott is an outspoken leader in an informal, uninstitutionalized network of minds dedicated to creating a New Age of world peace through free enterprise and personal transformation. Scott explains, "The term 'New Age' is still scary to many people. What it is is a collection of perspectives that synthesize the best of all world traditions and cultures into a personal philosophy

· which is truly beneficial for the society and the individual."

It is precisely this approach, whether labeled "New Age" or not, that is propelling the country through the entrepreneurial revolution. Scott asserts, "Entrepreneurship prevents America from becoming a stagnant society. It's why we can change and evolve as a nation."

After a close encounter with death, Marc Magor decided to give up hang gliding. He swore up and down he would never take the risk again. Months later, he was flying again *and* had started a new company, High Adventure Sports.

Entrepreneurship works the same way. Once you've tasted freedom, you can never return. For this reason, the kid with the lemonade stand becomes the teenager with a paper route, who becomes the student entrepreneur with a flourishing campus enterprise, who becomes a full-scale globe-trotting entrepreneur.

The entrepreneurial life is far more than a career; it is a way of life. It shapes your whole way of thinking. What you once saw as problems you now see as opportunities. For example, it could be that frustration over lack of good service and healthy food in restaurants moves you to start your own natural foods restaurant.

And 9-to-5? Ridiculous! While seasoned entrepreneurs do set defined boundaries on their work time in order to make time for family, friends, vacations, etc., the whole notion of time becomes very flexible. As an entrepreneur, you encounter peak experiences and bite-the-dust failures. You feel ostracism from uninspired or jealous people, yet you find kinship with other entrepreneurially minded people and friendships of a depth not usually found in the workplace.

The reason entrepreneurship is so intertwined with the daily life of an entrepreneur is that the same "right stuff" that makes for success in business makes for success in life. And vice versa.

Entrepreneurs come in more varieties than Baskin-Robbins. There certainly isn't just *one* life-style, either, especially as we enter the late '80s and '90s. Entrepreneurs are evident in every arena, from bakers to aeronautics designers to stock market analysts to floral designers. My mother Carolyn defies all the business stereotypes. Through her natural foods stores and seminars, she has helped transform thousands of lives.

No matter what arena you enter, you can be entrepreneurial. The corporation as we know it is disappearing, and some experts say it may be extinct by the millennium. It is being replaced by "intrapreneurs," individuals and small groups within larger corporations who are given as much capital and autonomy as they need to develop new ideas and products. In exchange, the profits of the enterprise are shared between the parent corporation and the intrapreneurs.

At the root of it all, "entrepreneur" is not a job title, or even an activity. It is an ability. It may sound strange, but everyone who undertakes an enterprise, whether profit or nonprofit, corporate or community, is an entrepreneur in the broadest sense of the word. Even if you do not pursue a career as an entrepreneur in the traditional sense, the training you get from being a student entrepreneur is valuable all your life. I learned about decision-making, managing finances, handling risk and uncertainty, and dealing with people far more through my business ventures than anywhere else. ACE members are urged to promote change and innovation within *any* organization they are involved in—from one's own business to schools, nonprofit organizations, corporations, and small businesses.

SOCIAL TRANSFORMATION THROUGH BUSINESS

"The young entrepreneur is clearly emerging as the nation's opinion leader," states ACE co-founder Verne Harnish. He adds that it's a proven fact that entrepreneurs are preferred as marriage partners. It is not difficult to imagine that one of our future presidents will emerge from today's group of young entrepreneurs.

It has long been known that the real seat of power in the U.S. is not in Washington, but in the business sector. (The other "golden rule": "Those who control the gold, make the rules.") Entrepreneurs number among those who make decisions that affect thousands. Along with this power comes a strong imperative to use it ethically.

Business ethics is not just some esoteric philosophical debate. You don't need to pull out Aristotle to decide whether you're going to cheat your customers or not. Any entrepreneur who has half a grain of sense knows that businesses fail almost instantly once word gets around that the establishment has even slightly unsavory business practices.

Socially responsible entrepreneurship goes beyond simple right and wrong. It is what Scott Mize calls "a statement of living principles." It has to do with using business as a

"Miss Wilson, please bring me your tired, your poor,
your huddled masses. . . ."

way to transform the world. It means instituting sound
business practices in every enterprise you undertake, from
a popcorn concession stand to a high-tech investment company. It means making practices like win/win, personal
responsibility, intensive communication, and teamwork/
synergy such standard habits that anything else would seem
primitive. (And besides, social responsibility results in a
healthier bottom line.)

The real driving force behind economic activity is the
desire to change things. For many, the change is simply
improving their economic status from poverty to riches.
For entrepreneurs, however, the desire has the flavor of

what Steve Jobs calls "passion for something you want to change—passion must drive entrepreneurship. . . . Money is just the booby prize." Brett Kingstone adds, "Money is not the ultimate goal, It's just a way of keeping score. Entrepreneurs are driven by dreams. My dream is to see commerce between countries promote world peace."

WHAT WEALTH REALLY IS

If money is just the "booby prize," as Jobs puts it, then why does everyone scrabble for it?

The key lies in the difference between *money* or *riches* on one side, and *wealth* on the other. Wealth, which means, literally, "well-being," encompasses a lot more than money. Wealth is health, knowledge, security, relationships, and emotional and spiritual wholeness. If it is used wisely, money can get you part of the way there, but it's still only the means, not the end. And in the case of entrepreneurship, it's the entrepreneurial passion and withstanding the trials-by-fire of entrepreneurship that ultimately achieves what money alone can't: A sense of fulfillment.

It may sound extreme, but I believe entrepreneurs have not only a right, but a *duty* to produce as much wealth as they can. Who can bridge the gap between idea and actualization, between opportunity and production, better than the entrepreneurial mind?

There's a catch, however. I believe that the emphasis should be on *producing* rather than on *hoarding*. The reason small entrepreneurial companies often beat the larger institutionalized corporations to the punch is that the latter are so busy guarding what they have that they don't have energy left for taking the initiative. For this, Apple Computer adopted one of Steve Jobs's favorite expressions: "The journey *is* the destination."

I also believe entrepreneurs have not only the duty to produce, but to produce appropriately. Appropriate production, or "appropriate technology," refers to using resources to create the greatest good for the greatest number of people. Wealth should be produced for the good of the community, not just for one or a few. This is a sharp departure from the more common idea that "producing wealth" is one and the same as "taking advantage of wealth," even to the extent of brutally exploiting others. You don't have to look far to see this perversion in action: South Africa's apartheid system is a mockery of liberty and free enterprise. Not only does it deny entrepreneurial opportunities to nonwhites, it effectively enslaves them. The relevance of this issue is: The same generation that produced the student entrepreneur movement was the same one that pressured American colleges and universities to remove themselves from such an insult to free enterprise.

It is exactly this spirit of simultaneous respect for free enterprise and social responsibility that gives this generation the opportunity to make concrete changes. This generation has more savvy and clout than the noisy voices of the late '60s and early '70s, thanks to improved education, better communications, and the computer revolution. It also has proven to have a stronger sense of applied responsibility than the head-in-the-sand cynicism of the late '70s and early '80s, as shown by a more serious attitude toward school, rising SAT scores, more realistic career plans, and the apartheid divestment movement. This generation is what the media are calling "pragmatic idealists."

Scott Mize is confident that, "Our generation will be the one to go a step beyond the examples of Mitch Kapor of Lotus Development Corporation and Steve Jobs and make the companies even better for the people."

A VISION FOR THE FUTURE . . .
AND WHERE WE ARE NOW

Buckminster Fuller, a visionary and a popular philosopher, calculated that if the world's resources, including human resources, were employed for maximum development and minimum waste, everyone on this planet would be a millionaire. In other words, everyone would enjoy the freedom and privileges that only a few enjoy today—all 5 billion of us.

The basis of Fuller's argument is what win/win is based on: We're playing an infinite-sum game, not a zero-sum game. That is, it isn't true that if you win, I lose. Rather, if I help you win, I win too. Instead of slicing up an economic pie of finite resources, entrepreneurs are out there creating *infinite* resources. The potential world economy is more like a magic pie that keeps replenishing itself from below . . . as long as creative entrepreneurial activity continues.

In today's service- and information-based society, we no longer can measure wealth or even economic activity in terms of material goods or even dollars. We're undergoing what Marilyn Ferguson, author of *The Aquarian Conspiracy*, calls a "paradigm shift," a completely new way to look at things.

The new paradigm is creativity. Marilyn Ferguson states, "Creative intelligence is the wealth of a modern society." In this new society, it doesn't matter so much what you have in your pocket—it matters what you have in your head. Verne Harnish confides, "The term 'entrepreneurship' is becoming a cliché. What we're entering is an Age of Creativity."

In my vision of a new world that entrepreneurial minds will create, I see schools that do not suppress the creativity that children naturally have. I see high schools that teach young people teamwork and co-competition rather than rewarding one-upmanship. I see universities offering curricula that combine theory with practice, along with courses and clubs that teach entrepreneurial skills. I see students from diverse backgrounds putting themselves through school by working on the things they genuinely like to do. I see a workplace where communication, transportation, and commerce are almost instantaneous, and where space travel is as easy as hopping on a jet. I see artists who enjoy creating, teachers who enjoy teaching, engineers who enjoy designing. I see a society with 100 percent full participation and employment—a testimony to the fulfillment of Buckminster Fuller's calculation.

Entrepreneurship today simply isn't an elitist game anymore; rather, it is a great populist movement. In the days of monopolistic robber baron capitalism, true free enterprise didn't really exist. Whether by law, prejudice, lack of access to capital, or lack of mental capital, the average person couldn't even jump up to the first rung of economic opportunity. Communism, with all its foaming at the mouth over capitalistic oppression, turned out to be an oppressor itself. It smothered (and continues to smother) the human spirit within the monopoly of a depersonalized state.

The reality is that the New Entrepreneurship is pulling the rug out from underneath the scions of both the Old Right and the Old Left. In America, progressive visionaries like Steve Jobs of Apple and Next, Inc., and Mo Siegel of Celestial Seasonings (and especially the whole graduating class of today's student entrepreneurs) prove one thing: it *is* possible to promote human values, cooperation, and community orientation within the context of a free enterprise system. In fact, the New Entrepreneurship promises to end the senseless conflict between Left and Right that has deterred this century's progress.

In various parts of Latin America, where Communist guerrillas on the left have pitched an ongoing, bloody conflict with equally repressive landowners on the right, a few progressive landowners have decided to give *true* free enterprise a chance. For example, when a coffee plantation owner in Guatemala let the workers buy stock ownership in the plantation, they stopped giving aid to the guerrillas. Instead they began guarding their new property with their very lives. It makes perfect sense. Think of it: Communism always has promised to let workers profit directly from their own labors and own their own means of production. Entrepreneurs have been doing this all along!

"Just how long has Dr. Wolk been teaching, anyway?"

Except that something's changed. In today's most progressive companies, the entrepreneur is not some absent owner at the top, but rather the whole team. The entrepreneurs are workers and the workers are the entrepreneurs. The more resourcefully they work together, the more wealthy they all become.

At the present time, we are far from this ideal and it will take a little longer to achieve because society in general is afraid of risk, afraid of change. Our generation represents a concrete hope that the crossover will continue. After all, student entrepreneurs know nothing else than profiting from their own labors, owning their own means of production, taking risks, and transforming a vision into reality. *You and I are part of the solution, not part of the problem.*

Together, the featured student entrepreneurs and I have presented a travelogue of our entrepreneurial experiences. Along the way we've found risk and reward, solitude and companionship, booms and busts, temporary failure from lack of commitment—and ultimate success from our dedication to a vision. Now you stand at the start of this great adventure.

Take the Journey.

APPENDIX A
Resources

Books

Batterson, Leonard A., *Raising Venture Capital: And Other Musings on Risky Business*. New Jersey: Prentice-Hall, 1986.

Bennett, Steven J., *Playing Hardball with Soft Skills*. New York: Bantam Books, 1986.

Crowe, Gregory D. and Crowe, Patrick H., *Money Grubbing: A Student's Guide to Part-Time Jobs and Self-Run Businesses*. Chicago: Chicago Review Press, Inc., 1983.

Drexler, K. Eric, *Engines of Creation*. New York: Doubleday & Company, Inc., 1986.

Drucker, Peter F., *Innovations and Entrepreneurship: Practice and Principles*. New York: Harper & Row Publishers, 1985.

Ferguson, Marilyn, *The Aquarian Conspiracy: Personal and Social Transformation in the 1980's*. Los Angeles, J. P. Tarcher, Inc., 1981.

Gazvoda, Edward A., Jr. and Haney, William M., III, *The Harvard Entrepreneurs Society's Guide to Making Money: Or the Tycoon's Handbook*. Boston: Little, Brown & Company, 1983.

Hawken, Paul, *The Next Economy*. New York: Henry Holt & Company, 1983.

Hill, Napoleon, *Think and Grow Rich*. North Hollywood: Wilshire, 1966.

Kingstone, Brett, *The Dynamos: Who Are They, Anyway?* New York: John Wiley and Sons, 1986.

————*The Student Entrepreneur's Guide*. New York: McGraw-Hill, 1988.

Mandino, Og, *The Greatest Salesman in the World*. New York: Bantam Books, 1974.

Naisbitt, John, *Megatrends: Ten New Directions Transforming Our Lives.* New York: Warner Books, 1983.

Peters, Thomas J. and Waterman, Robert H., *In Search of Excellence: Lessons from America's Best-Run Companies.* New York: Harper & Row Publishers, 1982.

Silver, A. David, *Entrepreneurial Megabucks: The One Hundred Greatest Entrepreneurs of the Last Twenty-Five Years.* New York: John Wiley & Sons, Inc., 1985.

——— *The Silver Prescription.* New York: John Wiley & Sons, Inc., 1987.

Vesper, Karl H., *Entrepreneurship Education 1985.* Wellesley: Babson College, 1986.

Waitley, Denis, *The Psychology of Winning.* New York: Berkeley Publishers, 1984.

Magazines and Newspapers

Business Week. 1221 Avenue of the Americas, Suite 4360, New York, New York 10020.

Entrepreneur Magazine. 2311 Pontius Avenue, Los Angeles, California 90064.

Forbes. 60 Fifth Avenue, New York, New York 10011.

Fortune. 1271 Avenue of the Americas, Rockefeller Center, New York, New York 10020.

Inc. 38 Commercial Wharf, Boston, Massachusetts 02110.

Success. 521 Fifth Avenue, New York, New York 10175.

Venture. 521 Fifth Avenue, New York, New York 10175.

The Wall Street Journal. 220 Battery Street, San Francisco, California 94111.

Other Resources

The American Entrepreneur Series: "I Can Do It." Ed Lewis, Stew Leonard, and Judi Wineland. A three-tape autobiographical series about young entrepreneurs. Directed by Laurie Kreindler-Laster, LKL Productions, Inc., in New York, majority funded by The National Federation of Independent Business Resources and Education Foundation in Washington, D.C.

Tape #1	Ed Lewis	1984
Tape #2	Stew Leonard	1985
Tape #3	Judi Wineland	1985

The series is available in VHS videocassette tapes and 16-mm projection film, English and Spanish, and can be viewed as the three-tape set or individually.

The Student's Guide to Earning Money. Bill Sanders, Nightingale-Conant Audiotapes, Chicago, 1983. This is an audiocassette program.

Nightingale-Conant Corporation
7300 North Lehigh Avenue
Chicago, Illinois 60648
Motivational tapes, books, etc. Write for brochure.

APPENDIX B
Entrepreneurial Ideas

The ideas in this section represent a collection generated from actual student businesses, brainstorming sessions at ACE at UCSD, and ideas that occurred to me while running, hang gliding, shaving, etc. To aid you, I've separated them into some rather arbitrary groupings according to academic interests.

Arts/Physical Education

- Put together a band of talented artists and do thematic murals on downtown buildings and freeway ramps. Start with a proposal at your own school and gain a reputation.
- Put together another talented group to paint Christmas themes on shopkeepers' windows during the Yuletide season
- Become a professional athletic trainer in your sport
- Organize an outdoor jazz festival on campus
- Open a fashion consulting service. This can thrive in cosmopolitan cities like Washington, D.C., Boston, etc.
- Design T-shirts or sweaters
- Create custom artwork and advertising for businesses
- Give art, music, or sports lessons
- Perform as a clown or musician
- Photograph weddings and special events
- Design and sew creative clothing for children
- Organize rock-climbing or whitewater trips
- Teach windsurfing, scubadiving, or underwater basketweaving
- Make or custom-paint skateboards or surfboards
- Be a house call masseur/masseuse (strictly legit, of course)
- Market your own line of cookies, fudge, or cakes
- Make or repair leather backpacks
- Create a mobile music DJ show
- Design a solar radiation dashboard protector with your school's logo

- Make and sell Christmas wreaths and similar holiday crafts
- Make a VHS movie for your school's admissions department
- Make a calendar of interesting/beautiful/infamous people or professors on your campus
- Design logos and posters
- Draw portraits at fairs, malls, etc.
- Open an aerobics dance studio
- Assemble a performance troupe (ballet, street theater, rock and roll band, etc.) and go on a national tour.

Biology/Chemistry/Health Sciences

- Explore microscope photography and electron micrography; make and market photos or posters on the head of a pin, the faces of sand fleas, etc.
- Organize a preventive medicine lecture for the public, featuring knowledgeable professors/professionals in your field
- Invent and market your own line of cosmetics and beauty aids
- Invent a cure (or better, a *prevention*) for AIDS and cancer
- Create or clone a pressure-resistant strain of grass. Replace every parking lot in America with natural living carpets you can park your car on.
- Turn the roof of a city apartment building into a producing garden, starting with your own. Combat smog, carbon monoxide, and urban blight with oxygen-exhaling plants.
- Wash, groom, exercise, or train pets
- Raise worms and fish bait
- Till gardens
- Grow and sell flowers or vegetables, especially pumpkins for Halloween
- Exercise and care for horses
- Open a greenhouse
- Engineer or clone new life-forms
- Invent a smog- or sewage-eating plant
- Dive for lobster, abalone, or pearls
- Raise truffles
- Invent and package a fire-retardant to spray on Christmas trees
- Raise bees and sell the wax or honey

- Invent and market aids for handicapped people, such as computer hardware and software for paraplegics, toys and crafts for the blind, visual "music" for the deaf. (The telephone was invented by accident; Alexander Graham Bell was looking for a way to communicate better with his almost-deaf wife!)

Computer Science

- Write educational software for preschoolers using extensive graphics; test it with your little brother or sister
- Teach programming or word processing classes; write your own electronic textbook for them
- Write software for untapped sectors of the market (e.g., first-timers initiated into the world of computers)
- Write a science fiction text-adventure with alternative outcomes
- Design decision-making aids for students choosing a major
- Act as a computer consultant to organizations and individuals
- Start a computer dating service with a creative twist
- Design and build interfaces for different computer systems
- Start a computer-based bulletin board system
- Invent and install computerized security systems
- Deal in used computer equipment
- Design flyers on your computer
- Design tutorials for physics students and text tutorials in any subject
- Write simulation software for the Big Bang Theory. What does your model predict about the birth and death of galaxies?

Economics/Business/Entrepreneurship Studies

- Pool cash with your parents or several other student entrepreneurs and buy investment property to live in while you're attending school. Why pay rent when you can sit on a nest egg instead?
- Start an investment club or hold an entrepreneurs' networking party
- Run a limousine service
- Buy and sell power boats
- Hire kids to collect hubcaps from streets and highways (hire only *honest* kids)
- Start a specialty radio station
- Compile a discount coupon book of local merchants

- Set up your little brother or sister in a lemonade stand
- Start a night janitorial company for businesses and institutions
- Start a student bank/investment/credit agency on campus
- Sell used records and tapes
- Sell blank cassettes and computer disks at a discount
- Charter buses for students returning home at Thanksgiving and Christmas
- Give motivational seminars or speeches
- Create an ice cream truck out of an old van
- Rent stunt kites, surfboards, Frisbees, etc., at the beach
- Rent or sell refrigerators, furniture, or posters to dormies
- Rent VCRs and answering machines
- Find a business partner in another country and set up an artisan's cooperative. Help set up these self-supporting communities in Latin America, Asia, and Africa by assuring them a market in the U.S. and Europe.

Humanities/English/Communications

- Write a magazine article about your entrepreneurship experiences
- Set up a student radio station on campus
- Start a newsletter/data base for student entrepreneurs in your region
- Establish a creative writing or arts magazine on your campus
- Begin an English tutoring service for foreign students
- Organize a Shakespeare festival or Renaissance Faire
- Tutor academics
- Write for magazines
- Type term papers
- Do fact-finding, research, and photocopying for undergrads, graduate students, and professors (and companies wishing to use university libraries)
- Create a guide to local party spots
- Start a magazine or newsletter
- Create a line of clever bumper stickers
- Start a lecture note service (with university permission)
- Travel the world, and later give a series of seminars or travelogues
- Write a pamphlet or on-line document for freshmen on what to expect in your major

- Write poetry and team up with a musician to put your "lyrics" to song. (Meanwhile, submit your original poetry for publication.)
- Write a book about some aspect of your college experience and get it published

Physics/Engineering

- Design an R & D project for the Space Shuttle
- Tune up bicycles, cars, motorcycles, or small engines
- Fix stereos and cassette players
- Build an experimental solar-powered (or wind-, water-, or wave-powered) house with several other engineering students
- Invent a light bulb that doesn't burn out
- Build and sell computers from kits
- Design an ingenious, low-cost water transport system for Third World countries. Publish the idea, and personally direct its implementation in a test community.
- Invent a device that neutralizes smog or precipitates it out of the air

"Your table is ready."

- ♦ Design a fourth generation Frisbee
- ♦ Invent hybrid sports equipment that combines the excitement of several sports. (Past examples include windsurfers, parasailing, snowboards, etc.)
- ♦ Build and sell huge or intricate clear plastic maze-cages for gerbil owners
- ♦ Invent a personal aircraft as an alternative to cars that is as light as a hang glider and as safe as a hot air balloon
- ♦ Invent a skydiving suit modeled after a flying squirrel, with membrane-like wings to retard the descent
- ♦ Invent a flexible rubberlike safety glass for windshields that absolutely will *not* cut flesh on impact
- ♦ Make and sell cars from kits, or design and market your own
- ♦ Repair small engines
- ♦ Start a custom phone-recorded weather report catering to surfers, pilots, boaters, etc.
- ♦ Invent and install solar pool heaters
- ♦ Make a windsurfer with wheels and other toys for grown-ups
- ♦ Build custom lofts in dorm rooms
- ♦ Make swingsets and children's toys
- ♦ Invent a new kind of kite or toy airplane
- ♦ Create a "Fantasy Island" service. For example, if your clients are into scubadiving, arrange an underwater ocean grotto stocked with coins and clues to the buried treasure. If the clients prefer a "West World" experience, rent a Hollywood set and hire extras to initiate bogus gunfights with your clients. Charge $500 to $10,000 per fantasy.

Political Science/Social Sciences

(Note to the reader: the ideas in this section have been placed here because they require leadership and organizational ability.)

- ♦ Open a genealogical research service
- ♦ Start a birthday surprise service
- ♦ Collect bottles and cans for recycling
- ♦ Throw a mud-wrestling party. Hire popular, good-looking characters or popular professors to take on all comers (the paying customers).

- ◆ Recycle scrap wood
- ◆ Throw a $50-a-plate bash on a chartered yacht the night of the college formal or a high school prom
- ◆ Organize a triathlon or other mega-event
- ◆ Set up a student travel service
- ◆ Start a "U-drink, we drive" taxi service
- ◆ Start an employment service
- ◆ Recycle newspaper into fireplace logs
- ◆ Employ teenagers to chaperone youngsters on Halloween night for parents who sign up and pay for the service
- ◆ Join forces with other young entrepreneurs who are currently submitting proposals to privatize the U.S. prison system, with an emphasis on rehabilitation for reentry into society.

Psychology/Education

- ◆ Begin a tutoring service
- ◆ Organize a positive-thinking rally
- ◆ Set up a CBBBS (computer-based bulletin board system) for teens as a forum to make contact and discuss their problems with each other
- ◆ Baby-sit and care for children
- ◆ Promote seminars and special events
- ◆ Aid senior citizens by providing home services or cooking meals
- ◆ Arrange children's parties and excursions
- ◆ Compile a data base of student course evaluations which rate professors' effectiveness.
- ◆ Run a day-care center or alternative camp
- ◆ Set up a nonprofit "adopt-a-freshman" program on your campus, linking up savvy juniors and seniors with members of the incoming class. Or set up an "adopt-a-grandparent" program linking up students with family-less senior citizens in their nursing homes or convalescent hospitals.

Other

- ◆ Employ jobless inner city teens to sweep sidewalks in front of the stores of paying clients
- ◆ Make and sell pastries or candy
- ◆ Open a concession stand at public events and parks

- Type invoices for businesses
- Make and sell novelty or gag gift items
- Wax surfboards
- Sell flowers and novelties at crowd events (loop-the-loop planes, sports-fan caps)
- Deliver gorilla-grams in a gorilla suit
- Make and sell pizza on campus
- Set up vending machines in public places (with permission)
- Cater private picnics in remote or romantic spots
- Make photo business cards
- Sell aerobics, Frisbees, and hackey sacks with public demonstrations
- Travel to other countries, importing their entrepreneurial ideas and adapting their inventions for use in the U.S.

Somebody ought to come up with a . . .

. . bicycle you can "pedal" with both arms and legs.

. . . computerized wake-up service. You could let your modem and voice synthesizer do the work while you snooze!

. . . "sequence for success" time management program for a lap computer.

. . lap computer that folds up to the size of a wallet or wristwatch.

. . holographic computer screen that projects three-dimensional images that move.

. . . custom portrait service using impressionable clay molds, with which you could make instant sculptures of the client's face.

. . national newsletter or data base of idea-orphans like these which inventors and entrepreneurs have chosen not to patent or develop.

. . . light, aluminum and dacron "bus" that can be pedaled around the campus or city.

I strongly believe no one "owns" ideas. (How could they, since two people on opposite sides of the globe can come up with the same idea simultaneously?) The truth is that ideas are unlimited. The best way to come up with them is to enter into a free and active interchange of ideas with other entrepreneurially minded people.

APPENDIX C
Business Plan and Budget

Business Plan Worksheet

This business plan is based on the ideas in Chapter 3. Skip whatever lines do not apply. Note that it will be hard to fill in all the specific figures in one sitting. Therefore, update it as you go along.

1. *Service or product*
2. *Goals*
   Sales volume   by (date)
   Achievements
3. *The entrepreneurial team*
   Key members
   Backgrounds and unique strengths
4. *Market*
   Characteristics of buyers
   Prices I will charge
5. *Competition*
   Names of other competitors
   What they offer and how much they charge
   Indirect competition
   My success ingredient
6. *Marketing plan*
   Distributorship
   Advertising
   Promotion opportunities
7. *Sales strategy*
   Type of sales force
   Selling strategy
   Sales quotas
   Commissions

8. *Management*
Division of responsibilities
Organizational procedures
Management philosophy and innovations

9. *Operations* (List specific needs applicable to you; save estimated costs for the budget worksheet.)
Business location
Fixtures
Services used

Raw material
Inventory
Names of suppliers, their prices, and their delivery policies
Tools and equipment

10. *Bookkeeping*
Type of system: single-entry, double-entry, software
Billing policy
Bank and type of accounts

11. *Legal*
Business license
Fictitious Business License (DBA)
Seller's permit
Zoning ordinances
Liability coverage and bonding
Tax schedules

12. *Timetable*
Make a schedule of goals and deadlines on a separate page.

13. *Financial projections*
Summary of operating budget
Amount of startup capital needed
Growth potential
Future financial plans

14. *Personal purpose*
Personal sacrifices, benefits, and work values
What will you do with the money?

Worksheet for an Initial Operating Budget

(Note: Using Chapter 4 as a guide, make photocopies of this sheet to begin your business/es.)

ESTIMATED EXPENSES
from (date) _____ to (date) _____

Equipment/tools .... _____

    Fixtures/rent .... _____

    Supplies/inventory .... _____

    Paid labor .... _____

    Advertising .... _____

    Legal fees/licenses .... _____

    Miscellaneous services .... _____

    Cash reserve .... _____

Subtotal of Expenses _____

    Amount of cash you personally have for

    capitalization .... _____

    Amount you need to borrow .... _____

Projected Income .... _____

    from (date) _____ to (date) _____ _____

Projected Profit .... _____

Acknowledgments

Thanks to:

My parents, Bruce and Carolyn

The fifteen featured students

The entrepreneurial team of ACE at UCSD

My encouraging, "no-limit" editor, Martha Lawrence

And:

Larry Aberman

Clint Albin

Gene Ashlock

Dr. James Belasco

Bob Dorn

Dr. Merrill Douglas

Gerald Dugan

Carmen and Jaime
Figueroa

Bill Gladstone

Tino Guzmán Khang

Verne Harnish

Kelly Horton

Karen Hutchinson

Roger Lane

John Ledden

Tonya MacDonald

Tom Mangee

Fritz Milhaupt

Dwight O'Neill

Lori Ramsey

Tony Robbins

Luz Sanchez

Bill Sanders

Robert J. Sturner

Dr. Karl Vesper

Dr. Denis Waitley

Ann Wawer

Harriet Whitfield

Jan Zupnick

About the Author

Van Hutchinson is a 23-year-old student entrepreneur whose enterprises have ranged from operating an organic lemonade stand at age six to writing a book as a high school senior project, *Excelling: High School Superstars and How to Become One*. He has published over 60 magazine articles, and gives seminars nationwide on entrepreneurship and student leadership. He recently finished his senior thesis at the University of California, San Diego, where he founded ACE at UCSD, an affiliate of the Association of Collegiate Entrepreneurs.

"Let's hear from that dumpy man with the thick glasses in the back row."

About the Illustrator

John Callahan is a 38-year-old cartoonist whose work regularly appears in the *New Yorker, National Lampoon, Omni, American Health, Penthouse,* and many newspapers, including the *Arizona Star* and the *San Francisco Chronicle.* He has been paralyzed from the chest down since 1972 (as a panel from one of his strips, "The Lighter Side of Being Paralyzed for Life," explains: "We ended the evening by driving the Volkswagen into a billboard at 90 miles an hour. Looking back on it, I kind of wish we hadn't done this.") In 1983 he graduated from Portland State University with a bachelor's degree in English and a coterie of admirers, who eagerly anticipated his new cartoons—usually drawn in class. He is a native of Portland, Oregon, where he currently lives with Lizzy and Watson, his cats.

CALLAHAN

"People like you are a real inspiration to me!"

Printed in the United States
6096

9 780156 191500